Contemporary Southern Poetry
AN ANTHOLOGY

Contemporary Southern Poetry

AN ANTHOLOGY

Edited by
Guy Owen *and* Mary C. Williams

LOUISIANA STATE UNIVERSITY PRESS
Baton Rouge and London

59464

Design : Dwight Agner
Typeface : Linocomp Gailliard
Composition : Briarpatch Press
Printing : Thomson-Shore, Inc.
Binding : John H. Dekker & Sons, Inc.

LIBRARY OF CONGRESS
CATALOGING IN PUBLICATION DATA

Main entry under title :

Contemporary Southern poetry.

1. American poetry—Southern States.
2. American poetry—20th century.
I. Owen, Guy, 1925–   II. Williams, Mary C., 1923–
PS551.C56   811'.5'408   79–13010
ISBN 0–8071–0577–5
ISBN 0–8071–0578–3 pbk.

The editors are grateful to the following authors, publishers, and periodicals for permission to reprint these poems.

Ann Arbor Review for "Ybor City" by Duane Locke.

Atheneum Publishers for "The Assassination" from *Departures*, copyright © 1973 by Donald Justice.

Atlantic Monthly for "Tobacco Men" by James Applewhite, copyright © 1977 by the Atlantic Monthly Company, Boston, Mass.

AURA Literary/Arts Review for "Washington on the Constitutional Journey : 1791" by Paul Baker Newman.

A. S. Barnes & Company, Inc. for "The Nude Poet" and "Squashes" from *The Man in the Green Chair*, 1977, by Charles Edward Eaton.

George Braziller, Inc. for "Victory" from *Welcome Eumenides*, copyright © 1972 by Eleanor Ross Taylor.

Broadside Press for "The Idea of Ancestry" from *Poems from Prison*, 1968, by Etheridge Knight; "A Poem for My Father" from *We a BaddDDD People*, 1970, by Sonia Sanchez.

Burnt Hickory Press for "Faith Healer Come to Rabun County" and "A Trucker Drives Through His Lost Youth" from *Jamming with the Band at the VFW* by David Bottoms.

Corinth Books for "A Dance for Militant Dilettantes," "A Dance for Ma Rainey," and "Birthday Poem" from *Dancing*, 1969, by Al Young.

Dark Tower for "A Bullfrog Pond Not Far from an Abandoned Farm" by Duane Locke.

Florida Review for "The Land of the Old Fields" by Van K. Brock.

The Fountain for "A Woman Combing" by William E. Taylor.

University of Georgia Press for "My Grandfather's Funeral" and "On the Homefront" by James Applewhite, from *Statues of the Grass*, copyright © 1975 by the University of Georgia Press; "Fish" by D. C. Berry, from *Saigon Cemetery*, copyright © 1972 by the University of Georgia Press; "Laurel and Hardy" and "Song of the Darkness" by John Bricuth, from *The Heisenberg Variations*, copyright © 1976 by the University of Georgia Press; "The Bee Woman" and "Squirrel Stand" by Jim Wayne Miller, from *Dialogue with a Dead Man*, copyright © 1974 by the University of Georgia Press.

David R. Godine, Publisher, for "The Mountain Cemetery" from *Living Together: New and Selected Poems*, copyright © 1956, 1965, 1973 by Edgar Bowers; "Carpenters" from *Steeplejacks in Babel*, copyright © 1973 by Turner Cassity; "Moving North" and "Basic Rescue" from *There Is No Balm in Birmingham*, copyright © 1972, 1974, 1975, 1976, 1978 by Ann Deagon.

Greenfield Review Press for "There Were Fierce Animals in Africa" from *Feeling Through*, 1975, by Alvin Aubert.

Harcourt Brace Jovanovich, Inc. for "The Migrants" and "The Peace of Wild Things," copyright © 1968 by Wendell Berry, and "Marriage" and "East Kentucky," copyright © 1967 by Wendell Berry, from *Openings*, 1968; "The Farmer Among the Tombs," copyright © 1969 by Wendell Berry, and "The Mad Farmer Revolution" and "Water," copyright © 1970 by Wendell Berry, from *Farming: A Hand Book*, 1970; "At the Birth of a Poet : Amherst, 1830," copyright © 1967 by Larry Rubin, and "Saturday Afternoon," copyright © 1963 by Larry Rubin, from *Lanced in Light*, 1967; "Burial," copyright © 1972 by Alice Walker, from *Revolutionary Petunias and Other Poems*, 1973, and "Hymn," copyright © 1968 by Alice Walker, from *Once*, 1968.

Holt, Rinehart and Winston for "Pachuta, Mississippi/ A Memoir" from *The Song Turning Back into Itself*, 1971, by Al Young.

Houghton Mifflin for "The Oceans of Dr. Johnson" from *Dr. Johnson's Waterfall*, 1946, by Helen Bevington, and "Nature Study, After Dufy" from *A Change of Sky*, 1956, by Helen Bevington.

Iris Press for "Afternoon" from *New and Selected Poems*, 1977, by George Scarbrough.

Jackpine Press for "My Grandmother Sifting" from *Out in the Country, Back Home* by Jeff Daniel Marion.

Alfred A. Knopf, Inc. for "Heaved from the Earth," from *Heaved from the Earth*, copyright © 1969, 1970, 1971, by Besmilr Brigham; "The Soup Jar" from *The Diving Bell*, 1966, by Dabney Stuart.

Larkspur Press for "The Poet Finds an Ephemeral Home in a Truck Stop on the New Jersey Turnpike" from *Getting It on up to the Brag*, 1975, by James Baker Hall.

Louisiana State University Press for "Southbound" and "Walking Out" from *Walking Out*, copyright © 1975 by Betty Adcock; "Cleaning the Well" and "My Grandmother Washes Her Feet" from *River*, copyright © 1975 by Fred Chappell; "February" from *The World Between the Eyes*, copyright © 1971 by Fred Chappell; "Pastoral" and "Lines to the South" from *Lines to the South and Other Poems*, copyright © 1965 by John William Corrington; "Kite" from *After Borges*, copyright © 1972 by R. H. W. Dillard; "Pity" from *Watch for the Fox*, copyright © 1974 by William Mills; "Hogpen," "Steep," and "Dark Corner" from *Land Diving*, copyright © 1976 by Robert Morgan; "At the Seed and Feed" from *Driving to Biloxi*, copyright © 1968 by Edgar Simmons; "The Ballad of the Volunteer" from *Round and Round*, copyright © 1977 by Dabney Stuart; "A Local Man Goes to the Killing Ground" from *Domains*, copyright © 1966 by James Whitehead; "Getting Experience" and "Why God Permits Evil" from *Why God Permits Evil*, copyright © 1977 by Miller Williams; "Let Me Tell You" from *Halfway from Hoxie*, copyright © 1977 by Miller Williams.

Macmillan Company for "To Live and Die in Dixie" and "A Humble Petition to the President of Harvard" from *Collected Poems, 1924–1974* by John Beecher; "Tenantry" by George Scarbrough from *Traveling in America*, ed. David Kherdian, 1977.

McDowell, Obolensky for "Woman as Artist" from *Wilderness of Ladies*, 1960, by Eleanor Ross Taylor.

University of Missouri Press for "For a Bitter Season," "Abraham's Knife," "Revival," and "Solitaire" from *For a Bitter Season: New and Selected Poems*, copyright © 1967 by George Garrett.

Moore Publishing Company for "That Summer" from *To the Water's Edge*, 1972, by Sam Ragan.

University of Nebraska Press for "Aunt Emma, Uncle Al: A Short History of the South" from *Dry Lightning*, 1960, by Marion Montgomery; "God Opens His Mail" and "The Runaway" from *The World's Old Way*, 1963, by Larry Rubin.

New Orleans Review for "Death" by John Stone.

New Yorker for "Cumberland Station" by Dave Smith, from *Cumberland Station* (University of Illinois Press), copyright © 1975 by New Yorker Magazine, Inc.

University of North Carolina Press for "To William Wordsworth from Virginia," "Rockland," and "A Ballad of Eve" from *The Puritan Carpenter*, copyright © 1965 by Julia Randall; "Dealer's Choice and the Dealer Shuffles," "The Ancient of Days," and "The Priapupation of Queen Pasiphaë" from *An Ear in Bartram's Tree*, copyright © 1969 by Jonathan Williams.

W. W. Norton & Company for "Hard Weed Path Going," "Corsons Inlet," "Silver," and "Unsaid" from *Collected Poems, 1951–1971*, copyright © 1972 by A. R. Ammons; "Topsoil" from *Red Owl: Poems*, copyright © 1972 by Robert Morgan.

Olivant Press for "I Must Come to Terms with Florida" from *Devoirs to Florida*, 1968, by William E. Taylor.

Poets in the South for "Bellair" by Van K. Brock and "Going Under" by Ann Deagon.

Random House, Inc. for "For a Woodscolt Miscarried" by John William Corrington, from *Contemporary Poetry in America*, ed. Miller Williams, 1973.

Rutgers University Press for "Resuscitation" by John Stone, from *The Smell of Matches*, copyright © 1972 by Rutgers University, the State University of New Jersey.

Sewanee Review for "The Ceremonies" by Van K. Brock, first published in the *Sewanee Review* LXXXII (Summer, 1974). Copyright © 1974 by the University of the South.

Smith/Horizon Press for "Skimmers" from *The Ladder of Love*, 1970, by Paul Baker Newman.

Southern Poetry Review for "Surviving the Wreck" by Betty Adcock; "Balls and Chain" by Alvin Aubert; "We Let Each Other Go" by Coleman Barks; "Moby Christ," "Barriers 1," and "Barriers 2" by Gerald Barrax; "Kilroy Turtle" by D. C. Berry; "The New Dolores Leather Bar" by Turner Cassity; "Of Jayne Mansfield, Flannery O'Connor, My Mother and Me" by Rosemary Daniell; "York Harbor Morning" by George Garrett; "The Poet Finds an Ephemeral Home in a Truck Stop on the New Jersey Turnpike, ca. 1970" by James Baker Hall; "The Dawn Horse," "To Redound," "Literacy: An Abandoned Ode," and "Mothsong" by William Harmon; "The Schloss" and "The Briefing" by David Kirby; "Jim Worley Fries Trout on South Squalla" by Jim Wayne Miller; "The Advent Images" and "A Snowman in March" (from *In an Ordinary Place*) by Paul Ramsey; "Snake Sermon" and "Two Memories of a Rented House in a Southern State" by Dave Smith; "He Makes a House Call" by John Stone; "The Flying Change" by Henry Taylor; "About a Year After He Got Married He Would Sit Alone in an Abandoned Shack in a Cotton Field Enjoying Himself" by James Whitehead.

University of Texas Press for "This Cold Nothing Else" from *Blood, Hook & Eye*, 1977, by Dara Wier.

Texas Tech Press for "Impromptu Immersion in Tom's Run" from *Reeds*, 1978, by Gibbons Ruark.

Trident Press, a Division of Simon and Schuster, Inc., for "My South" and "Zeppelin" from *Damned Ugly Children*, 1966, by Andrew Glaze.

University of Utah Press for "Buildings and Grounds" and "Speech" from *An Afternoon of Pocket Billiards* by Henry Taylor.

University of Virginia Press for "Sleeping Out with My Father" and "A Blind Wish for Randall Jarrell" from *A Program for Survival*, 1971, by Gibbons Ruark.

Wesleyan University Press for "Cherrylog Road," "The Heaven of Animals," "The Performance," "The Shark's Parlor," and "Adultery," copyright © 1960, 1961, 1963, 1966 by James Dickey, from *Poems—1957–1967*; "Cherrylog Road," "The Heaven of Animals," and "The Shark's Parlor" first appeared in *New Yorker*.

Contents

Introduction

It has become a cliché in commentaries on the South, New South, or Sunbelt, that the region has lost its distinctiveness and has been absorbed into the mainstream of America. We are even told that we can no longer speak of a southern sensibility. Yet anyone who looks at our literature is immediately struck by differences, sometimes subtle but often obvious enough, that set us apart from the rest of the nation. For instance, there is the southern language that colors our fiction or the southern novelists' emphasis on racial themes and narratives centered around the family. Though less readily apparent, the same distinctiveness can be observed in the poetry of our region, which is currently undergoing a dynamic development.

This ferment in southern poetry, which we observed during twenty years of editing *Southern Poetry Review*, has led to the present anthology, the first comprehensive collection since World War II. In addition to the richness and assured craftsmanship that have been undervalued or have gone unnoticed, we want to illustrate both the diversity which is now strongly characteristic of this poetry and also the evidence of a recognizable southern tradition.

We believe that it is not contradictory to speak of the variety in the poetry of our region while maintaining that we discern a southern tradition. But before identifying the characteristics of this tradition, perhaps we should point out as one argument for its existence that most of the sixty-four poets we have included wish to be known as southern, although they realize the limitations of being termed regionalists. In an informal survey of many of them, we found them emphasizing their southernness. Only one poet objects that the whole issue is a dead horse which ought to be buried. More characteristically, Fred Chappell writes, "I've always lived in the South. I'd be a pure fool to sell my birthright for a mess of 'universality.'" According to Jim W. Miller, "The mountain South is the only place that, as a poet, is 'alive' for me, the only place I know almost by instinct. But I am not, and don't wish to be, ignorant or unmindful of other places or times. So I try . . . to receive everything that comes from outside the region in such a way as not to overwhelm the regional but rather to act as a stimulus for the regional." David Bottoms, like others, speaks of a rich southern heritage: "As Southerners, we have a terribly colorful, beautiful, and awesome culture to draw on. We're tremendously lucky." Nor do poets reject the South even when their feelings about it are ambivalent: "I find that my love-hate relationship with my region creates much of the energy for my writing," says Rosemary Daniell, reminding us of Faulkner or Thomas Wolfe.

In our postwar poetry the most authentic material deriving from this heritage is rural life, especially smalltown communal life. (Many southern poets still think of the South as being agrarian.) And if a reader should object that what we are describing is rural poetry, not simply southern poetry, we might agree. Yet we are unaware of poetry from any other region of the United States today that exhibits so prominently and consistently the same cluster of attributes. One does not need to elaborate on the southerner's attachment to place or his clinging to the Jeffersonian myth. The title of Jeff Daniel Marion's book, *Out in the Country, Back Home*, would apply to much of the best work of a number of poets. The natural scene of a variety of regions is rendered with care and attention to realistic detail: for example, Virginia by Julia Randall, Texas by Betty Adcock, Kentucky by Wendell Berry, Georgia by James Dickey, and Florida by William E. Taylor.

In addition to its rural subject matter, another characteristic of this poetry is a noticeable conservatism in forms and techniques, seen here, for instance, in Jim W. Miller's sonnet "Squirrel Stand" or the disciplined quatrains of Vassar Miller's "The Ghostly Beast." Ballads are still being written in the South, to say nothing of villanelles and cinquains, though free verse prevails.

Thirdly, there is our distinctive language. As is the case with other regions, the characteristic language of the South is disappearing under the flattening effect of TV and the educational system. Yet it is often possible to perceive a southern flavor in our poetic diction. Certainly many of these poets are aware of the different layers of language still available to them (note, for instance, Fred Chappell's "Dropping like a meteor, / I cried aloud—"Whoo! It's *God Damn* cold!—dancing the skin of the star" in "Cleaning the Well"). As one would expect, dialect no longer plays a major role, as was the case with the local colorists or later writers of regional fiction, but occasional localisms add vividness to the poetry of the seventies from the mountain idiom of Robert Morgan to the low country Carolina talk of James Applewhite or the Deep South black speech of Al Young. But, as a rule, our poets prefer a mixture of the formal and colloquial rather than a return to the outmoded dialect poem.

Southern poets also tend to rely heavily on concrete, sensuous images—images are at the center of our folk speech—though of course the region is not the only one to nourish such poems. It is a truism of the southern mind that it disdains abstractions and tends to focus on specifics. One recalls John Crowe Ransom writing that he "started with a fury against the abstract." And Walter Sullivan has noted, "The Southerner saw the world and its history as a series of images rather than as a sweep of theories, which is to say that his vision was not abstract, but concrete." Thus, although a poet like A. R. Ammons often delights in abstractions, the most characteristic approach of the poets represented here can be observed in the sharpness and density of the images in Robert Morgan's "Toolshed" or James Dickey's "Cherrylog Road." One can assume that the South will not soon produce an "imageless" poet such as Robert Creeley.

The country of these poets is often the country of memory; in this, again, they resemble novelists like Wolfe and Faulkner. But today the past is seldom romanticized. Instead, it is treated with realism, irony, and humor. No doubt it is appropriate that this collection leads off with Betty Adcock's "Southbound," a memory poem which begins, "You can go back. . . ." Most of these authors can go back, and for some, it seems, they are compelled to go home again. This is as true for black poets as white; witness Etheridge Knight's "The Idea of Ancestry" or Alice Walker's "Burial." Not only do they feel that they have roots in a particular southern place (place-names abound in their poems), but they have a strong sense of community with the people of that place. They want to tell stories about it, as do Miller Williams in "Getting Experience" and James Dickey in "The Shark's Parlor." There is often humor in their narratives and an obvious affection. Time and time again we are reminded that the South is still a region of storytellers.

On the other hand, there are inevitable rebels for whom a southern heritage is cause for anger and pain. Andrew Glaze's contempt for southern hypocrisy in "My South" exemplifies the nature of such rebellion, as does Rosemary Daniell's anger at Milledgeville, Georgia, the town that "murders women." Charles Wright's "Northhanger Ridge" ("Sunday, and Father Dog is turned loose") illustrates the turning away from traditional religion and the church.

In fact, one of the chief differences between the Old South and the New South is the increased secularization of life and thought. This contrast is easily seen by comparing the poems in Addison Hibbard's anthology *The Lyric South* (1928), which contains an important section labeled "The Searching Spirit," and this anthology in which there are only a handful of poems expressing simple, unaffected piety. Poems that appear to have religious subjects often turn out to focus more on man than on God, or they may employ religion for local color rather than inspiration. Of course, this is not to say that spiritual feeling is no longer a shaping force in southern letters, but it is no longer clearly Christian.

Perhaps one further observation might be risked: southerners have habitually valued a sense of wholeness in all aspects of their art. It might be said, then, that southern poets are more likely to stress design and continuity rather than the fragmentary and disjunctive. This emphasis on wholeness and order, which may be a further aspect of our conservatism, becomes apparent when one compares a southern poet with, say, the current New York School.

One reason many of our poets may feel free to be southern, rather than simply American, is that they are not competing with predecessors of towering reputations as southern novelists are. Referring to William Faulkner's work, Flannery O'Connor said that "nobody wants to be caught on the tracks when the Dixie Special comes through." The case of poetry is dramatically different, for, as Allen Tate commented in 1932, "The historian of Southern poetry must constantly pause to enquire into the causes of our thin and not very comprehensive performance." Donald Davidson and H. L. Mencken concurred in his evaluation. The poems of Timrod and Lanier or those in *The Lyric South* will not overwhelm any reader, nor has their subject-matter been exhausted. In his introduction Addison Hibbard put his finger on the cause: "In comparison with the poetry of the country as a whole, the product of the Southern poets strikes one as strangely satisfied with things as they are. It is, in a very real sense, a lyric South concerned with beauty and emotional ecstasy almost to the exclusion of anything like actuality."

Although the southern poets represented here have generally tossed out ecstasy and concentrated on actuality, their world is not the same as that of contemporary southern novelists. Perhaps poets feel that the novelists have appropriated some of their potential themes. The Civil War, for instance, makes little appeal to poets today. The agony of racial prejudice is one of the primary subjects for blacks, but white poets seem drawn to it less frequently than white novelists, who are, of course, depicting a society as well as individual experience. Though contemporary poets treat the rural landscape and the smalltown community, they do not usually feature Tobacco Road sharecroppers, mental retardation, or sexual depravity. They refrain from obscene language, as a rule, and seldom deal very directly with sex. In these ways the materials of southern poetry differ from southern fiction, which until recently has tended to overshadow our poetry.

There is, of course, no secret about why southern poetry has suddenly come out of the shadows and demanded recognition. For the first time we have a generation of poets which is truly professional—and with the aid of our Poetry-in-the-Schools programs, we may soon have an audience worthy of them. About two-thirds of these poets are college professors, who are not only writers but teachers, critics, and often translators of poetry. They are helping to create the climate in which their art can flourish.

An inevitable result of this situation is a concentration of academic poets. If in *The Lyric South* "the emotions squeezed out the intelligence," as Hibbard conceded, the intellectual approach of Ransom and Tate has often resulted in poems that have a brittle and dry quality, especially in the work of their students and imitators. In the poems of college-based poets of the fifties one notices the repetition of themes and allusions, as well as tightly controlled diction and rhythms and a fashionable ironic stance. Since the Beat movement, however, there has been a rebellion in the South—and elsewhere—against the Fugitives, who had earlier repudiated Poe and Lanier. The well-wrought ironic poem has been brought into question, along with the whole approach to literature of the New Critics. As one young southern poet commented of the Fugitives, "Hell, all those guys grew up on farms, but how many wrote poems about gutting a hog or priming tobacco?" Although the academic tradition is being continued by poets as skillful as Charles Edward Eaton and Donald Justice, recent southern poetry is more relaxed, colloquial, down-to-earth, and accessible than that of the Fugitives and their followers. It is also far more varied.

By refusing to swim in schools or arrange themselves in convenient categories, southern poets are exhibiting a diversity and an independence not previously observed. Such generalizations as we have been making are qualified by numerous poems and several of the poets in this book. Larry Rubin's poems or William Harmon's, for instance, are not local and not specifically southern. Blacks may write of race, jazz, prison, and dope—or anything else. We do not want what we suggest here to be construed as limiting or distorting the vision of any writers.

In the poems that follow we have tried to illustrate the impressive variety of southern poetry: the witty and crisp light verse of Helen Bevington, the meditative and tentative poems of A. R. Ammons, the narratives of Fred Chappell or James Dickey, the ecological poems of Wendell Berry, the protest poems of John Beecher, and the "deep image" poems of Duane Locke. The feminist movement, not yet strong in the South, is represented by Rosemary Daniell. We include, too, the powerful black voices of Alice Walker, Gerald Barrax, Al Young, Sonia Sanchez, Alvin Aubert, and the prison poet Etheridge Knight. By contrast, the section entitled "The Negro" in *The Lyric South* did not include a single black poet, for black writers before World War II felt compelled to leave the South. Today, though black writers may be living elsewhere, they seldom want to abandon their southern identity. Sonia

Sanchez, born in Alabama but for some years a resident of the Northeast, writes: "Yes! I still consider myself a Southern poet. Indeed!" A new diversity of tones, styles, and themes, then, characterizes southern poetry in the sixties and seventies.

Finally, a note on our principles of selection. In order to emphasize what is new, we have limited the poets represented, with few exceptions, to those who began publishing since the Second World War. One of our hardest decisions was to leave out the Fugitives altogether. Certainly any collection of southern poetry would be much stronger with representative poems from Allen Tate, Robert Penn Warren, John Crowe Ransom, and Donald Davidson. However, the work of these old masters is readily available in numerous collections, as well as in their own Fugitive anthology. In fact, we find that the Fugitives have tended to eclipse a whole generation of poets in the South for whom we hope to find a wider audience. Perhaps this alone is enough to justify a new anthology.*

We have faced a number of other hard decisions. One was to leave out poets who are no longer actively publishing; another was to exclude those who have not published at least one book of poems. Randall Jarrell will be especially missed here, though he wrote very few poems that might be identified as southern.

More difficult still, since there is obviously no certified test for "southernness," was to decide which native southerners to include who have lived elsewhere for many years, and which poets to include who were born elsewhere but now live in the South. Our solution was to admit only a few non-native-born poets. Further, nearly all of these few moved to the South well before maturity, and most of their writing has been done here. On the other hand, a number of poets who have moved away—like A. R. Ammons, who teaches at Cornell, and George Garrett, who now lives in Maine—we claim as southern because their sensibilities have been shaped by the region, their work often speaks of it, and, in fact, they look on themselves as southern. Unfortunately, these decisions have required us to leave out memorable poems by Heather McHugh, Robert Watson, John Haines, Hollis Summers, and Peter Meinke, to cite only five accomplished poets.

* There have been other anthologies since Addison Hibbard's *The Lyric South*, published in 1928, but not very comprehensive ones. In 1962 Guy Owen and William Taylor edited a chapbook of original poems, *Southern Poetry Today*. Frank Steele collected the work of twenty-three new poets in *Poetry South-East: 1950–70*. In 1967 Miller Williams and John William Corrington edited *Southern Writing in the 60's: Poetry*, but their small volume seems like an afterthought to their more ambitious anthology of southern fiction. *New Southern Poets*, edited by Guy Owen and Mary C. Williams in 1974, included only poems previously published in *Southern Poetry Review*; *White Trash*, edited by Robert Waters Grey and Nancy Stone in 1977, included no black writers.

It should be obvious that the editors have aimed at an eclectic volume, and one in which most of the poets are represented by two to four poems. We have not wanted to favor any particular school, style, or region— though we readily admit to the usual academic bias against the romantic poetry fostered by poetry societies and the "folksy" verse expected of our poets laureate. (These types of verse are, to be sure, still very much with us.) Though we selected a few poems for their subject matter—hunting, fishing, a tobacco market, a revival meeting—we have not tried to exemplify a black-eyed peas and grits school of verse, nor did we want a book that would display a narrow provincialism.

It is our hope that this anthology makes our case that contemporary southern poetry, while diversified, has an enduring tradition that is central to its success and that this tradition is one of energy, strength, and poetic craft. As southern as most of these poems are, we like to think that they succeed, first and foremost, as interesting and memorable poems.

Guy Owen and Mary C. Williams

Contemporary Southern Poetry
AN ANTHOLOGY

Southbound

You can go back in a clap of blue metal
tracked by stewardesses with drinks and virginal masks.
These will work whether you breathe or not. And this
is the first part. The way is farther
into thin roads that sway with the country.
Through the shine of a rented car the red towns rise
and crumble, leaving faces stuck to you like dust.
Following the farms, houses the color of old women,
you gather a cargo from yards full of lapsed
appliances, tin cans, crockery, snapped wheels,
weedy, bottomless chairs. These float through the air
to rest on the sleek hood, the clean seats.
Things broken out of their forms
move to you, their owner, their own.
You slow under weight. The windshield blurs
with the wingbeat of chickens. The hound's
voice takes over your horn.
A green glass vase from a grave in a field
comes flowerless to your hand, holds a smell
of struck matches, of summer on rust, of running
water, of rabbits, of home.

Then the one place flung up like a barrier,
the place where you stop, the last
courthouse and gathering of garrulous stores.
You have brought the town.
It walks in your skin like a visitor.
Here, under the wooden tongue of the church,
by the paths with their toothed gates,
in the light of the drunk as he burns
past hunkered children reaching
for the eyes of their fathers, these fading
and coming like seasons,
you are the tall rooms of your dead.

Merchants still ring small furious bells
and the window of the moviehouse opens,
and the girls who will, open.
Men still stand jack-knifed to trace

deer trails in the dirt.
And blacks scythe the lawns, not singing,
keeping their flag hidden.

You may house again these weathers worn thin
as coins that won't spend, worn smooth
as the years between two who are old
and not fooled any longer. You may stand
beneath the cafe's blue sign where it steps
on the face like a fly. You may bend
to finger the cracked sidewalk,
the shape of stilled lightning, every fork
the same as it was when you thought that map
led to the rim of the world.

You may listen for thunder.

Walking Out

Fishing alone in a frail boat
he leaned too far, lost hold,
was turned out of the caulked world.
Seventy years he had lived without learning
how surfaces keep the swimmer up.

In that green fall, the churn of fear
slowing to pavane,
one breath held precious and broken,
he counted oar-strokes backward:
shore was not far.
This coin he took from the pocket of terror.

Starting over, over his head,
he reached for the earth.
As creatures of water once called on the future
locked in their bodies, he called on his past.
He walked. Walked. And there was enough
time, just enough, and luck.
Touching greenfingered sand, rising and touching,
body bursting with useless knowledge,

he came at the world from its other direction
and came to his place in air.

Back in his life now, he measures
distances one breath long,
talks less, flexes
the oars of his legs.

> Things shimmer where he is,
> his house, his earthcolored wife and sons.
> Every place raises walls around him
> the color of old glass.
> Heaven is a high clear skin.

Beneath the drift of flesh his bones remember
trying for bottom.

Surviving the Wreck

My body holds crazed messages I can't remember,
what the spirit sees when its weather
breaks and the blank moment scatters.
Only a cornfield dark with rain
or, intimate and deep, the roots' upheaval
or close, the white bone rammed
out of its packet.

Three days disappeared. The tree of impact
grew full, forgotten under my skin.
Hospital windows opened on a field,
three horses grazing the early light.
Waking was fierce, wordless and plain.

This tree of scars inside me like a child
turns to the dirty window-light that holds
love's dust, our wars, this growing old:
three horses grazing in a field of sun.
Waking is fierce and simple, and goes on.

A. R. Ammons

Hardweed Path Going

Every evening, down into the hardweed
going,
the slop bucket heavy, held-out, wire handle
freezing in the hand, put it down a minute, the jerky
smooth unspilling levelness of the knees,
      meditation of a bucket rim,
lest the wheat meal,
floating on clear greasewater, spill,
down the grown-up path:

      don't forget to slop the hogs,
      feed the chickens,
      water the mule,
      cut the kindling,
      build the fire,
      call up the cow:

      supper is over, it's starting to get
dark early,
better get the scraps together, mix a little meal in,
nothing but swill.

      The dead-purple woods hover on the west.
I know those woods.
Under the tall, ceiling-solid pines, beyond the edge of
field and brush, where the wild myrtle grows,
      I let my jo-reet loose.
A jo-reet is a bird. Nine weeks of summer he
sat on the well bench in a screened box,
a stick inside to walk on,
      "jo-reet," he said, "jo-reet."
      and I
would come up to the well and draw the bucket down
deep into the cold place where red and white marbled
clay oozed the purest water, water celebrated
throughout the country:
      "Grits all gone?"
      "jo-reet."
Throw a dipper of cold water on him. Reddish-black
flutter.

"reet, reet, reet!"

Better turn him loose before
cold weather comes on.
            Doom caving in
            inside
            any pleasure, pure
            attachment
            of love.

Beyond the wild myrtle away from cats I turned him loose
and his eye asked me what to do, where to go;
he hopped around, scratched a little, but looked up at me.
Don't look at me. Winter is coming.
Disappear in the bushes. I'm tired of you and will
be alone hereafter. I will go dry in my well.
            I will turn still.
Go south. Grits is not available in any natural form.
Look under leaves, try mushy logs, the floors of pinywoods.
South into the dominion of bugs.

            They're good woods.
But lay me out if a mourning dove far off in the dusky pines
            starts.

            Down the hardweed path going,
leaning, balancing, away from the bucket, to
Sparkle, my favorite hog, sparse, fine black hair,
grunted while feeding if rubbed,
scratched against the hair, or if talked to gently:
got the bottom of the slop bucket:
            "Sparkle . . .
            You hungry?
            Hungry, girly?"
blowing, bubbling in the trough.

            Waiting for the first freeze:

"Think it's going to freeze tonight?" say the neighbors,
the neighbors, going by.

            Hog-killing.

Oh, Sparkle, when the axe tomorrow morning falls
and the rush is made to open your throat,

I will sing, watching dry-eyed as a man, sing my
      love for you in the tender feedings.

She's nothing but a hog, boy.

Bleed out, Sparkle, the moon-chilled bleaches
      of your body hanging upside-down
hardening through the mind and night of the first freeze.

Corsons Inlet

I went for a walk over the dunes again this morning
to the sea,
then turned right along
   the surf
         rounded a naked headland
         and returned

   along the inlet shore:

it was muggy sunny, the wind from the sea steady and high,
crisp in the running sand,
     some breakthroughs of sun
   but after a bit

continuous overcast:

the walk liberating, I was released from forms,
from the perpendiculars,
     straight lines, blocks, boxes, binds
of thought
into the hues, shadings, rises, flowing bends and blends
      of sight:

        I allow myself eddies of meaning:
yield to a direction of significance
running
like a stream through the geography of my work:
  you can find
in my sayings
        swerves of action

like the inlet's cutting edge:
there are dunes of motion,
organizations of grass, white sandy paths of remembrance
in the overall wandering of mirroring mind:

but Overall is beyond me: is the sum of these events
I cannot draw, the ledger I cannot keep, the accounting
beyond the account:

in nature there are few sharp lines: there are areas of
primrose
    more or less dispersed;
disorderly orders of bayberry; between the rows
of dunes
irregular swamps of reeds,
though not reeds alone, but grass, bayberry, yarrow, all . . .
predominately reeds:

I have reached no conclusions, have erected no boundaries,
shutting out and shutting in, separating inside
    from outside: I have
    drawn no lines:
    as

manifold events of sand
change the dune's shape that will not be the same shape
tomorrow,

so I am willing to go along, to accept
the becoming
thought, to stake off no beginnings or ends, establish
    no walls:

by transitions the land falls from grassy dunes to creek
to undercreek: but there are no lines, though
    change in that transition is clear
    as any sharpness: but "sharpness" spread out,
allowed to occur over a wider range
than mental lines can keep:

the moon was full last night: today, low tide was low:
black shoals of mussels exposed to the risk
of air
and, earlier, of sun,

waved in and out with the waterline, waterline inexact,
caught always in the event of change:
   a young mottled gull stood free on the shoals
   and ate
to vomiting: another gull, squawking possession, cracked a crab,
picked out the entrails, swallowed the soft-shelled legs, a ruddy
turnstone running in to snatch leftover bits:

risk is full: every living thing in
siege: the demand is life, to keep life: the small
white blacklegged egret, how beautiful, quietly stalks and spears
      the shallows, darts to shore
         to stab—what? I couldn't
      see against the black mudflats—a frightened
      fiddler crab?

         the news to my left over the dunes and
reeds and bayberrry clumps was
      fall: thousands of tree swallows
      gathering for flight:
      an order held
      in constant change: a congregation
rich with entropy: nevertheless, separable, noticeable
      as one event,
            not chaos: preparations for
flight from winter,
cheet, cheet, cheet, cheet, wings rifling the green clumps,
beaks
at the bayberries
   a perception full of wind, flight, curve,
   sound:
   the possibility of rule as the sum of rulelessness:
the "field" of action
with moving, incalculable center:

in the smaller view, order tight with shape:
blue tiny flowers on a leafless weed: carapace of crab:
snail shell:
         pulsations of order
         in the bellies of minnows: orders swallowed,
broken down, transferred through membranes
to strengthen larger orders: but in the large view, no

lines or changeless shapes : the working in and out, together
      and against, of millions of events : this,
         so that I make
         no form
         formlessness :

orders as summaries, as outcomes of actions override
or in some way result, not predictably (seeing me gain
the top of a dune,
the swallows
could take flight—some other fields of bayberry
        could enter fall
        berryless) and there is serenity :

      no arranged terror : no forcing of image, plan,
or thought :
no propaganda, no humbling of reality to precept :

terror pervades but is not arranged, all possibilities
of escape open : no route shut, except in
    the sudden loss of all routes :

      I see narrow orders, limited tightness, but will
not run to that easy victory :
        still around the looser, wider forces work :
        I will try
    to fasten into order enlarging grasps of disorder, widening
scope, but enjoying the freedom that
Scope eludes my grasp, that there is no finality of vision,
that I have perceived nothing completely,
      that tomorrow a new walk is a new walk.

Silver

    I thought Silver must have snaked logs
      when young :
she couldn't stand to have the line brush her lower hind leg :
in blinded halter she couldn't tell what had loosened behind her
      and was coming
as downhill

to rush into her crippling her to the ground:

and when she almost went to sleep, me dreaming at the slow plow,
I would
at dream's end turning over the mind to a new chapter
     let the line drop and touch her leg
     and she would
bring the plow out of the ground with speed but wisely
fall soon again into the slow requirements of our dreams:
how we turned at the ends of rows without sense to new furrows
and went back
     flicked by
     cornblades and hearing the circling in
the cornblades of horseflies in pursuit:

  I hitch up early, the raw spot on Silver's shoulder
sore to the collar,
get a wrench and change the plow's bull-tongue for a sweep,
and go out, wrench in my hip pocket for later adjustments,
     down the ditch-path
by the white-bloomed briars, wet crabgrass, cattails,
     and rusting ferns,
riding the plow handles down,
  keeping the sweep's point from the ground,
the smooth bar under the plow gliding,
the traces loose, the raw spot wearing its soreness out
in the gentle movement to the fields:

     when snake-bitten in the spring pasture grass
Silver came up to the gate and stood head-down enchanted
     in her fate
I found her sorrowful eyes by accident and knew:
nevertheless the doctor could not keep her from all
the consequences, rolls in the sand, the blank extension
     of limbs,
     head thrown back in the dust,
useless unfocusing eyes, belly swollen
wide as I was tall
and I went out in the night and saw her in the solitude
     of her wildness:

but she lived and one day half got up
and looking round at the sober world took me back

into her eyes
and then got up and walked and plowed again;
mornings her swollen snake-bitten leg wept bright as dew
and dried to streaks of salt leaked white from the hair.

Unsaid

Have you listened for the things I have left out?
I am nowhere near the end yet and already
     hear
     the hum of omissions,
the chant of vacancies, din of

silences:

there is the other side of matter, antimatter,
     the antiproton:
     we
have measured the proton: it has mass: we
have measured the antiproton: it has negative mass:

you will not

hear me completely even at this early point
unless you hear my emptiness:
     go back:
     how can I
tell you what I have not said: you must look for it

yourself: that

side has weight, too, though words cannot bear it
out: listen for the things I have left out:
     I am
     aware
of them, as you must be, or you will miss

the non-song

in my singing: it is not that words *cannot* say
what is missing: it is only that what is missing
     cannot

be missed if
spoken: read the parables of my unmaking:

feel the ris-

ing bubble's trembling walls: rush into the domes
these wordy arches shape: hear
       me
    when I am
silent: gather the boundaried vacancies.

My Grandfather's Funeral

I knew the dignity of the words:
"As for man, his days are as grass,
As a flower of the field so he flourisheth;
For the wind passeth, and he is gone"—
But I was not prepared for the beauty
Of the old people coming from the church,
Nor for the suddenness with which our slow
Procession came again in sight of the awakening
Land, as passing white houses, Negroes
In clothes the colors of the earth they plowed,
We turned to see bushes and rusting roofs
Flicker past one way, the stretch of fields
Plowed gray or green with rye flow constant
On the other, away to unchanging pines
Hovering over parallel boles like
Dreams of clouds.

                At the cemetery the people
Surprised me again, walking across
The wave of winter-bleached grass and stones
Toward his grave; grotesques, yet perfect
In their pattern: Wainwright's round head,
His bad shoulder hunched and turning
That hand inward, Luby Paschal's scrubbed
Square face, lips ready to whistle to
A puppy, his wife's delicate ankles
Angling a foot out, Norwood Whitley
Unconsciously rubbing his blue jaw,
Locking his knees as if wearing boots—
The women's dark blue and brocaded black,
Brown stockings on decent legs supporting
Their infirm frames carefully over
The wintry grass that called them down,
Nell Overman moving against the horizon
With round hat and drawn-back shoulders—
Daring to come and show themselves
Above the land, to face the death
of William Henry Applewhite,
Whose name was on the central store

He owned no more, who was venerated,
Generous, a tyrant to his family
With his ally, the God of Moses and lightning
(With threat of thunderclouds rising in summer
White and ominous over level fields);
Who kept bright jars of mineral water
On his screened, appled backporch, who prayed
With white hair wispy in the moving air,
Who kept the old way in changing times,
Who killed himself plowing in his garden.
I seemed to see him there, above
The bleached grass in the new spring light,
Bowed to his handplow, bent-kneed, impassive,
Toiling in the sacrament of seasons.

Tobacco Men

Late fall finishes the season for marketing:
Auctioneers babble to growers and buyers.
Pick-ups convoy on half-flat tires, tobacco
Piled in burlap sheets, like heaped-up bedding
When share-cropper families move on in November.

No one remembers the casualties
Of July's fighting against time in the sun.
Boys bend double for sand lugs, bowed
Like worshippers before the fertilized stalks.
The rubber-plant leaves glared savagely as idols.

It is I, who fled such fields, who must
Reckon up losses: Walter fallen out from heat,
Bud Powell nimble along rows as a scat-back
But too light by September, L. G. who hoisted up a tractor
To prove he was better, while mud hid his feet—
I've lost them in a shimmer that makes the rows move crooked.

Wainwright welded the wagons, weighed three
Hundred pounds, and is dead. Rabbit was mechanic
When not drunk, and Arthur best ever at curing.

Good ol' boys together—maybe all three still there,
Drinking in a barn, their moonshine clearer than air
Under fall sky impenetrable as a stone named for azure.

I search for your faces in relation
To a tobacco stalk I can see,
One fountain of up-rounding leaf.
It looms, expanding, like an oak.
Your faces form fruit where branches are forking.
Like the slow-motion explosion of a thunderhead,
It is sucking the horizon to a bruise.

A cloud's high forehead wears ice.

On the Homefront

I

Plate glass gazed on the depot. Auto parts wholesale.
Air brakes' coughs in switchyards, odor of metal.
A vacuum draws me: the wake of my father's words.

Nothing would be well said or ill, for order was by number:
So little part for me to play, I seem not present
In the memory.
                    Down the known aisles shelved to their ceilings,
We'd break upon a cave of mechanics, who bent in surrounding
Some motorblock open like a sacrificed carcass: hapless,
Greased. Plates and containers were set everywhere.
Unpalatable fluids. The point of the calendars was pictures,
Pin-up poses, nipples like the fuses of shells
Or nacelles of aircraft. An *artist's conception*. She reflected
Blessings onto hoods from the enameled tones of her limbs.

II

Preparation of a meal of oil. Everyone
Wiping his hands with mill waste, secretly pleased.
She on the calendar curved sleeker than metal.

The sizes of bolts were language.
These pale inner-temple mechanics, during daylight,
Practiced the refinement of cylinder and piston.

Balls and Chain

except for the heavy shoes and stout chains
these might just as well be the legs
of tropical lizards
the yeast of the mind would have it so
the spirit seeking a finer thing
than the crumbly buckshot soil
this part of georgia

who are these men whose faces
we do not see are they creatures
of striped legs only of bending backs
and beneath the uniformity of these rags
what song does heart sing to heart
soul to weary soul what benison
tends their calloused feet at the end
of a hot georgia day what soothing hand
helps to ease their burden down
what hand?

There Were Fierce Animals in Africa

there were fierce animals in Africa,
their king a noble white savage who swung
across a continent on a plaited vine.
that was before hemingway gave me
my first lesson in the mysteries of
kilimanjaro. even before i heard water
dance to the syncopated beat of
the congo. not to mention that lake
dutifully and ceremoniously dubbed
victoria. from whose enthronement
in colonized black minds all bounty
was taught to flow. there were all
these things and more in Africa.
but no people. no people.

even the mau mau was nothing
but a mean abstraction. a sundown
dance viewed from a cool veranda.

Coleman Barks

We Let Each Other Go

So the wedding guest, unknown
witnessing girl,
secretary, brought in at the last minute,
cried for both of us
in a courthouse office.
She cries in the kitchen, she cries
in her afternoon nap
twelve years later,
the same tears that married us.

I wander out in the backyard
with bedroom slippers on
in late spring
that moisture may touch me
on each foot.

Beings, constant movement.
We die, we let each other go, we meet,
we can barely hear.

In a glass case, a two-inch seated figure
like my own embryo,
Egyptian priest, absorbed in copying.

Here a girl who stretches in me
from toes to ears,
so I keep touching myself, lips,
ankle, smelling the skin on my wrist
as if I were my own lover.

This morning, when I seem
to cut my life in two,
and start the new count,
another notebook,
having gotten to twelve thousand
eight hundred and three,
I begin at one.

A blade down the middle
and two halves open
in the skinny mirrors of a knife.

Gerald Barrax

Moby Christ

Again, Father,
I've tried to escape the tyranny of your right hand—
how many times among those fools who never know me
until it's too late
and now as lord of these hosts of the waters.

Again, Father,
you've searched me out—
once Judas
and now the divine madness of an old man
to hound me down to the sea like an animal.

My scars multiply:
you'll fill my skin with harpoons
as you've filled my memory with your crosses—
what I must pay
to put spirit into flesh,
to feel, God, to feel
even the pain.
You are old, Father,
a fond and foolish old man
who has never known that much
about what you've created.

    My hosts will pay, too.
Men believe I once died for their sins
and now these great creatures will die for mine:
    there go the ships, Father,
on your wide sea which your wanton boys
will wash in Leviathan's blood
and hunt down to extinction.

When the sea gives up its dead
Father
will nothing rise from its depths
but the fools who have crawled over the earth?

Barriers 1

What does it mean
that there is a snake lying among the wild strawberries;
    Spring has laid smooth stones
      at the edge of the pool;
      there are birds who see farther at night
        than the warm things under cover of purple leaves?
Some god has bitten this mottled apple.
We swim in these summer days, its juices.
What does it matter where the snake hides:
    I was out of place until a blue jay
    in return for my seed
    left that black banded feather from his wing
    in my back yard.

Barriers 2

    After rain has cooled the rough skin
    Breathing eases
    And lungs, needles and leaves
    Go in and out into the air, ex-
    Changing molecules between me and the world,
    The power in that fire
    Moving live substances through our systems
    Like creatures below water's tension—
    Corpuscles oxygenating the sap,
    The tingling of photocells
    Synthesizing sunlight in the blood.
        Such darkness there was
        before the rain
        will come
    To feed the root systems out of the heart
    And send the love in the bowels
    Up the shaft of that power
    To these leaves flaming their tips
    Out into air again.

John Beecher

To Live and Die in Dixie

I

Our gang
laid for the kids from niggertown
We'd whoop from ambush chunking flints
and see pale soles
of black feet scampering
patched overalls and floursack pinafores
pigtails with little bows
flying on the breeze
More fun than birds
to chunk at
Birds
were too hard to hit

II

Old Maggie's sweat would drip and sizzle
on that cast iron range she stoked
but she was grinding at the handle
of our great big ice cream freezer
that day she had her stroke
It put a damper on my mother's luncheon
All the ladies in their picture hats and organdies
hushed up until the ambulance took Maggie off
but soon I heard
their shrieks of laughter
like the bird-house at the zoo
while they spooned in
their fresh peach cream

III

Asparagus fresh from the garden
my dad insisted
went best on breakfast toast with melted butter
so Rob was on the job by six
He used to wake me whistling blues
and whistled them all day till plumb
black dark when he got off
Times Mother was away

he'd play piano for me
real barrelhouse
(I liked it better than our pianola classics)
and clog on the hardwood floor
Rob quit us once to paper houses on his own
but white men came at night and sloshed
paint all over his fresh-papered walls
took the spark plugs out of his Model T truck
poured sand into the cylinders
then screwed the plugs back in
so when Rob cranked it up next day
he wrecked the motor
He came back to work for us
but I can't seem to remember
him whistling much again

IV

Black convicts in their stripes and shackles
were grading our schoolyard
At big recess we watched them eat
their greasy peas off tin
a tobacco-chewing white man over them
shotgun at the ready
and pistol slung
In class we'd hear them singing at their work
"Go Down Old Hannah"
"Jumpin Judy"
"Lead Me to the Rock"
I found a convict's filed off chain once in the woods
and took it home
and hid it

V

Tired of waiting for Hallowe'en
Jack and I had one ahead of time
and went round soaping windows
and chunking clods of mud on people's porches
Mr. Holcomb though came out shooting
his 45

at us scrouged up against a terrace
across the street
He meant to kill us too
because his fourth shot hit betwixt us
not a foot to spare each way
so we didn't wait for him to empty the magazine
but just aired out a mile a minute
Next day
our mothers made us apologize
and Mr. Holcomb said he wouldn't have shot at us
except it was so dark
he took us for nigger boys

VI

Confederate veterans came to town
for their convention
and tottered in parade
while Dixie played and everybody gave the rebel yell
but the Confederate burying ground near school
where the battle had been
nobody seemed to care about
It was a wilderness of weeds and brambles
with headstones broken and turned over
The big boys had a den in there
where they would drag the colored girls
that passed by on the path
and make them do
what they said all colored girls
liked doing
no matter how much
they fought back and screamed

VII

The Fourth of July
was a holiday for everybody but people's cooks
Corinne was fixing us hot biscuit
when I marched into the kitchen
waving the Stars and Stripes
and ordered her to
"Salute this flag! It made you free!"

I just couldn't understand why Corinne
plumb wouldn't

VIII

Old Major Suggs
ran for Public Safety Commissioner once
orating against the black menace
from his flag-draped touring car
and got just 67 votes
from a town that had 132,685 people in 1910
Things were well in hand back then
and folks were hard to panic
One night a chicken thief got into
old Major Suggs' hen-house
and made off with some of his Barred Rocks
The Major was slick
and figured out the path the thief was sure to take
back to niggertown
so he took a short cut through the woods
and hid behind a tree
The thief came staggering
beneath his sack of hens
and caught both barrels in his face
point-blank
"That nigger flopped and flopped"
old Major Suggs gloated long afterwards
"just like a big black rooster that you've axed"

IX

Spurgeon would daub designs on flowerpots
wheelbarrows
garbage cans
just anything he could get his hands on
though all he had was house-paint
and the kind of big flat brush
you slap it on with
My mother said
Spurgeon was what you call
a primitive
One Saturday evening

he was downtown window-shopping the pawnshops
gawking at all the jewelry
the pretty knives and pistols
when a mob came tearing round the corner
after another black man
but they made Spurgeon do

A Humble Petition to the President of Harvard

I am, sir, so to speak, "a Harvard man."
In legendary times I lugged my green
baize bag across the Yard to sit while fierce
Professor Kittredge paced his podium
in forkéd snowy beard and pearl-gray spats,
mingling his explications with his views
obscurantist on life and letters. Texts
prescribed for us were caponized. Prince Hamlet
made no unseemly quips anent the thighs
Ophelia spread for him nor did that poor
crazed beauty sing the naughty songs for which
she's celebrated. Nice young men were we
in Kitty's class. Extra-curricular
our smut—Old Howard queens of bump and grind,
the Wellesley girls who warmed our chambers. Such
the Harvard I recall: Widener's great hive,
whose honeyed lore we rifled and bore off
on index cards, all nutriment destroyed:
the home of Henry Wadsworth Longfellow;
dank mournful halls; an ill-proportioned pile
commemorating boys who'd marched away
to die for causes the professors had
endorsed, knowing infallibly which side
God and their butter were upon. Our boot-
legger was Polish. Christened Casimir
Zwijacz he'd changed his name to Lawrence Lowell
after fair Harvard's president. Ambushed
and shot by high-jackers who coveted
his rot-gut load, Lowell barrelled his truck

back from Cape Cod and, bandaged bloodily,
made punctual deliveries to all
his Cambridge clientele, fresh lustre shed
upon an honored name. *Per aspera!*
Nostalgic reminiscences brought on
by your most recent bulletin. I learn
of your "Commitment to the Modern," penned
expressly for Old Grads by Lionel
Trilling, D. Litt., a masterpiece, I thought,
of academic prose, so clear and yet
so dark. It cheers me that you do not change
at Harvard, like *castrati* whose voices
retain their boyish purity. Trilling
delights me with his cadenced double-talk.
"The radical," says he, and dares to add
"subversive" in a breathless tone, is like
to be predominant among the forces of
our time. Already on the student mind
(so impatient of the rational) this force
works powerfully. Oppose it, counsels he,
in order that it may grow strong and strike
deep roots. "Bland tolerance," he trills, "subverts"
subversion, makes it wither on the vine.
The way to nurse dissent is to impose
conformity—the logic's Lionel's—
and carefully exclude dissenters from
the faculty. Would we aid William Blake
to mew his mighty youth? Deny stipends.
Give ninnies suck at Alma Mater's teats.
Wean Blake. Choose Doodle in his stead as Poet
in Residence lest William be suborned
by excess of ease and lick the arses that
require booting. The University
of Hard Knocks is the proper berth for such
obstreperous geniuses. "When we are scourged,
they kiss the rod, resigning to the Will
of God," as Swift observed of moralists
like Trilling. Fend from me, I beg you, sir,
offers of chairs magnates endow. Waylay
me with no teaching sinecure (Degrees
sufficient to impress the Dean are mine.)

Summon me never to recite my verse
before a convocation in my honor
nor to appear in doctoral costume
as orator at Commencement. Such coddling,
as Trilling rightly says, would work my ruin.
Let me forever cope with penury
and cold neglect. Let me be ostracized
for practising ideals you fine folk
are given to prating of at ceremonies.
Do what you please with me defunct. Put up
a plaque. Dissect my corpse in seminars.
Transmogrify my bones to index cards.
Hang my dead portrait in the library
and crucify your living rebels still.

D. C. Berry

Fish

—poetry reading

Before I opened my mouth they sat as orderly
as frozen fish in a package.

Though I didn't notice it until it reached my ears,
water began to fill the room.

Then I heard sounds fish make in an aquarium.

Though I had tried to drown these students
with my words, theyhad opened up for them
like gills and let me in.

Together we swam around the room until the bell rang,
puncturing the door, where we all leaked out.

They went to another class, I suppose,
and I went home, where Queen Elizabeth,
my cat, met me and licked my fins
till they were hands again.

Kilroy Turtle

The nurse in the rainbow
Dress dances like her breasts
Are as untouched as the palm
Of the world's newest surgical glove.

Were I Dr. Kilroy instead
Of just Kilroy, S.O.B.,
I'd be very important and snug
Her as closely as water
Hugs rock apples,

My rubbery fingers
Fumbling ten soft roots
For a grip on the world,

My tongue ready to leap,

A trout,
Out of my mouth
Into the very whorl itself;

Instead, I'm Kilroy Turtle
And don't come out and that
Quickly her smile is gone
As she walks by and smiles.

Wendell Berry

The Migrants

They depart from what they have failed
to know—old clearings overgrown
with thicket, farmlands mute
under the breath of grazing machines.

Broken from the land, they inherit
a time without history, a future
their fathers did not dream of
and they do not imagine.

Where their fathers took the hill land
the forest returns. Rains usurp the hearths.
The fear of loss dies out
as the sills drift and sink.

The Mad Farmer Revolution

Being a Fragment
of the Natural History of New Eden,
in Homage
To Mr. Ed McClanahan, One of the Locals

The mad farmer, the thirsty one,
went dry. When he had time
he threw a visionary high
lonesome on the holy communion wine.
"It is an awesome event
when an earthen man has drunk
his fill of the blood of a god,"
people said, and got out of his way.
He plowed the churchyard, the
minister's wife, three graveyards
and a golf course. In a parking lot
he planted a forest of little pines.
He sanctified the groves,
dancing at night in the oak shades
with goddesses. He led

a field of corn to creep up
and tassel like an Indian tribe
on the courthouse lawn. Pumpkins
ran out to the ends of their vines
to follow him. Ripe plums
and peaches reached into his pockets.
Flowers sprang up in his tracks
everywhere he stepped. And then
his planter's eye fell on
that parson's fair fine lady
again. "O holy plowman," cried she,
"I am all grown up in weeds.
Pray, bring me back into good tilth."
He tilled her carefully
and laid her by, and she
did bring forth others of her kind,
and others, and some more.
They sowed and reaped till all
the countryside was filled
with farmers and their brides sowing
and reaping. When they died
they became two spirits of the woods.

On their graves were written
these words without sound:
"Here lies Saint Plowman.
Here lies Saint Fertile Ground."

The Farmer Among the Tombs

I am oppressed by all the room taken up by the dead,
their headstones standing shoulder to shoulder,
the bones imprisoned under them.
Plow up the graveyards! Haul off the monuments!
Pry open the vaults and the coffins
so the dead may nourish their graves
and go free, their acres traversed all summer
by crop rows and cattle and foraging bees.

East Kentucky, 1967

What vision or blindness lives
here among the broken places
in the smell of burning
and the stench of dead streams
where only machines thrive
on the death of all else?
What vision or blindness
can live in the sight of children
who inherit the eyes of broken men,
and in the sight of farms torn open
where the rich lock like toads
to the backs of the helpless?

Marriage

TO TANYA

How hard it is for me, who live
in the excitement of women
and have the desire for them
in my mouth like salt. Yet
you have taken me and quieted me.
You have been such light to me
that other women have been
your shadows. You come near me
with the nearness of sleep.
And yet I am not quiet.
It is to be broken. It is to be
torn open. It is not to be
reached and come to rest in
ever. I turn against you,
I break from you, I turn to you.
We hurt, and are hurt,
and have each other for healing.
It is healing. It is never whole.

The Peace of Wild Things

When despair for the world grows in me
and I wake in the night at the least sound
in fear of what my life and my children's lives may be,
I go and lie down where the wood drake
rests in his beauty on the water, and the great heron feeds.
I come into the peace of wild things
who do not tax their lives with forethought
of grief. I come into the presence of still water.
And I feel above me the day-blind stars
waiting with their light. For a time
I rest in the grace of the world, and am free.

Water

I was born in a drouth year. That summer
my mother waited in the house, enclosed
in the sun and the dry ceaseless wind,
for the men to come back in the evenings,
bringing water from a distant spring.
Veins of leaves ran dry, roots shrank.
And all my life I have dreaded the return
of that year, sure that it still is
somewhere, like a dead enemy's soul. Fear
of dust in my mouth is always with me,
and I am the faithful husband of the rain,
I love the water of wells and springs
and the taste of roofs in the water of cisterns.
I am a dry man whose thirst is praise
of clouds, and whose mind is something of a cup.
My sweetness is to wake in the night
after days of dry heat, hearing the rain.

Helen Bevington

The Oceans of Dr. Johnson

I never take a cup of tea
But I consider pleasurably
That, poured a twenty-seventh cup,
Dr. Johnson drank it up.

Before that mighty thirst was quenched,
Pot by pot, his hostess blenched
And, marveling, took fearful count
To be exact in the amount.

Perhaps his dryness had diminished,
Say, when the twenty-first was finished,
Yet being in a social mood
He drank to thrust out solitude,

Extending the complacent hour,
The festive rite, by staying power,
And twenty-seven cups would be
His limit, his capacity.

Nature Study, After Dufy

*When a friend accused Dufy of playing
fast and loose with nature,
he replied: "But nature, my dear Sir,
is only an hypothesis."*

I must remember to dismiss
These wintry skies that seem to me
Not gray, like an hypothesis,
But silver, like reality—
This arguable wind that stirs
So plausibly the conifers.

From postulates of days, unwary,
By seeming snows preoccupied,
I have conjectured January
And whiteness in the countryside,

Presumed the starlings in the holly.
I must remember now as folly

What earlier instants of surmise?
(The earth, one green and passing minute,
The poplar gold before my eyes,
The summer beech with sunlight in it—
These that by leaflessness of bough,
By empty fields, are proven now

Untenable, as soon must be,
With the first inference of spring,
This crystal world, this theory.)
I must be quick in questioning
The look of April after this
When it too is hypothesis.

David Bottoms

Faith Healer Come to Rabun County

Seldom is the tent full, but tonight he expects the local radio
to draw a crowd, also the posters up for weeks
in barber shop windows, beauty parlors, convenience groceries.
Even now his boys are setting out extra folding chairs,
adjusting the P. A. for more volume, less distortion,
wheeling the piano down the ramp of a U-Haul trailer.

In the back of a red Ford van he goes over his notes
on the healing power of faith:
the woman of Canaan whose daughter was rid of a devil,
the lunatic healed who fell no longer into fires,
the Sabbath healing of the withered hand,
the spitting into the eyes of the blind man of Bethsaida
who first saw men walk as trees
and then after the laying on of hands, men as men
walking on legs among the trees.

Even now he can smell the sweat, the sawdust, the reviving salts,
feel the healing hysteria run electrically through charged hands,
hear the quivering lips babble senselessly into the piano music.
Who would be healed, he will say, must file to God's altar
and stand in awe at the laying on of hands,
or those unable to be in the congregation
need only lay a hand on the radio,
withered as the hand may be it will be whole.

And if all goes as he prays it will go
even the most feeble will quake down the sawdust aisle,
kneel or fall unconscious at his shocking touch
to rise strong, young, healed in the spirit.
There is medicine in the passionate heart, he will say.
There is medicine in the power of God's love.
O Jesus, Savior, touch this sick brother
who accepts in faith the things we cannot know
O sisters come to the altar, lay your hands on the radio.

A Trucker Drives Through His Lost Youth

Years ago he drove a different route.
Hauling in a stripped-out Ford
the white hill whiskey nightclubs paid good money for,
he ran backroads from Ballground to Atlanta
with the cunning of a fox,
hung on each county's dirt curves like a banking hawk.

He remembers best how driving with no headlights
the black Ford felt for the road like a bat,
and how his own eyes, groping at first for moonlight,
learned to cut through darkness like an owl's.
Sometimes he drove those black roads on instinct alone.

As the shadow of a bridge falls across his face,
his rear-view says he is not the same man.
Still tonight when there is to traffic, no patrol,
no streetlamps to cast shadows or light the center line,
he will search again for the spirit
behind the eyes in the rear-view mirror.
Tonight in open country in heavenly darkness
the interstate to Atlanta will crumble into gravel and sand,
median and shoulder will fall into pine forest,
and his foot will floor the stripped-out Ford
till eighteen wheels roll, roll, roll
him backwards as far as his mind will haul.

Edgar Bowers

The Mountain Cemetery

With their harsh leaves old rhododendrons fill
The crevices in grave plots' broken stones.
The bees renew the blossoms they destroy,
While in the burning air the pines rise still,
Commemorating long forgotten biers,
Whose roots replace the semblance of these bones.

The weight of cool, of imperceptible dust
That came from nothing and to nothing came
Is light within the earth and on the air.
The change that so renews itself is just.
The enormous, sundry platitude of death
Is for these bones, bees, trees, and leaves the same.

And splayed upon the ground and through the trees
The mountains' shadow fills and cools the air,
Smoothing the shape of headstones to the earth.
The rhododendrons suffer with the bees
Whose struggles loose ripe petals to the earth,
The heaviest burden it shall ever bear.

Our hard earned knowledge fits us for such sleep.
Although the spring must come, it passes too
To form the burden suffered for what comes.
Whatever we would give our souls to keep
Is only part of what we call the soul;
What we of time would threaten to undo

All time in its slow scrutiny has done.
For on the grass that starts about the feet
The body's shadow turns, to shape in time,
Soon grown preponderant with creeping shade,
The final shadow that is turn of earth;
And what seems won paid for as in defeat.

John Bricuth

Laurel and Hardy
FOR LARRY AND FAITH

I

wide tie, wing collars, vest, and derby hats—

                                                          "don't

you kick *me* in the shin"—that spiff
boiled front of salad days—"you . . .
keep your distance"—the thin and the fat
ruined gentleman aiming a delirious
Ford with a broken knee, huffing
an upright piano
ten flights up,
fishing off a dock—"tell me,
why can't *we* ever get ahead"—
on the bum
               in the soup
(fish peddlers, Foreign Legionnaires),
battling against the odds to keep odd jobs,
say "Easy Come, Easy Go,"
slipping a bull fiddle to a Pullman berth,
hey, I was in the war, Mac—yeah, ya big "Beau Hunks,"
the race for their hats in the street's high wind,
politest before a fight—
                                what is it fulfills expectation?—
hearing the cuckoo march, we
anticipate
              the primness in Ollie's Danish pastry fingers
testing the tip of a punched nose,
the miffed wince when cops call him, "Fatty," say
        "move along, Fatty,"
the fluttered tie and tiny smile, the helpless
"why don't you do something to *help* me?" or
"here's another nice mess . . . ,"
know
Stanley's shovel-footed gait, half-moon grin,
in danger of falling
asleep, telling the truth—"don't you *dare*
touch that ladder"—leaning
head on hand
to miss completely

40

II

but, in fact,
Laurel was the brains of the team,
cold, aloof, English,
a fierce woman-chaser, married eight times,
demanding always twice Hardy's salary,
while Babe,
who'd dance like a bear
for biscuits and honey,
thought (faint drawl and courtly manners)
his real life started at forty-five
> when,

> > marrying,

he found untrue what he had believed for years—
no woman could love a fat, comic man

III

what is real?

Arthur Stanley Jefferson

> and Norvell Hardy?

these two and their two roles make four
and those four one where
playing his opposite each
defeats the other

> close your eyes—

there is the light-involving frame full
of a motion that is like music, discontinuous
yet finding its continuity in us, frame
supplanting, unmaking frame as note
displaces note
in movements of ablative grace

> we

are the dark interpreters of the lighted square,
taught to see two dimensions as three, taught
to feel depth as time and time as depth,
the music plays itself out in us

O
melodic and relentless demolition—
ties clipped, pants ripped—who falls
through the chimney to the basement
bringing the house down with him yelling
"wohoohohoo OH!" and sits
till the last brick drops "pock"
on his head—
                    to be
what it is about,
                    to be used up

these lives are the self-dissolving counterpoint
the music plays itself out in us

                    IV

that Ollie spent his last three years in a wheelchair,
paralyzed, unable to speak, the aristocratic
acrobat's lightness gone, light
dying on a coarsened face,
that Stanley and his last wife tried to live
in a beachfront apartment (dingy
with the bright sunlight of Santa Monica)
on a monthly government check
proves only
true lives are lived
                    moment to moment
by those
helpless to settle accounts
or save
        money,
                    themselves, since these
end
    with nothing,
                    or very little,
beyond the perfected gesture
                            and the stance

what is true? suppose
someone says, what is true?

say,
      the truth is time
devours his sons,
and say,
each moment slays the one before,
its father,
and in turn, is slain

Song of the Darkness
FOR ZELDA FITZGERALD

Beneath a striped umbrella
Whose brown sunlight is rain,
My colors melt and run.
There's an old ache in my brain.

Set your face in a smile—
Rough grains within a glass
Will char the fragile neck.
The sick never get well.

What was the tune I laughed?
Just once I knew myself
Falls before the leaf
Broke the sun in half.

Darling, why don't you come?
We could waltz, and whirling, you
Would forget words they say,
Loving the steps I do.

Strands of the musical stave,
Twisted with spikes of time,
Score the white throat.
My wires catch and sting.

Who said it was ill
to love by giving pain?
If time cures the sick,
The sick never get well.

Besmilr Brigham

Heaved from the Earth

after the tornado, a dead moccasin
nailed to the pole
boards scattered across a pasture

lying fierce crosses
jagged in mud

had flung itself
nail and wood
the square-headed animal
hurled also in air

or as it raced in weeds
)water flowing, water falling
impaled
      both the snake and timber
went flying through with wind

coiled, made a coil (they do
immediately from danger or when hurt
and died in a coil
bit itself
in pain of its own defense the poison

                  birds
                  hurled into yard
                  fences
                  one with feet tangled gripping
                  the open wire, a big Jay

struggling from the water
throwing its fanged head
high at the lightning, silent
in all that thunder

to die by its own mouth
pushing the fire thorns in

Van K. Brock

The Land of the Old Fields

After the latest mass murders
police scan infrared maps
for "hot spots" radiated
by decaying bodies;
they lug geiger counters
through abandoned fields listening
to the idiotstuttering, where
arrowheads lie on the ground
near bricks made by slaves,
and the names of slaveholders
who hunted Indians for bounty
are still hallowed in schoolbooks
shining with blood.

Large cats know in their paws
where they are by the felt
currents of underground rivers.
The earth has voice prints
I cannot hear even when I lie
near my father's house
with my best ear to the ground.

Snakes, cold-blooded,
spend their waking lives regulating
body temperatures. Deaf,
they hang their tongues in the night
to measure the slightest concussions
of air flowing into their mouths;
their scales decipher sound.
At night they are drawn like blood
to the best conductors:
large rocks that remember the
noon sun, new grave slabs.

Fossils and tooled stones litter
Apalachee.
"Tallahassee"—from Seminole—
the land of the old fields;
"Seminole"—from Creek—
they who went to a new place;

from
   "cimarron"—American Spanish—
   wild, runaway;
from
   "maroon"—French—
   runaway slave;
"A'palachi"—from Choctaw—
the people on the other side.
Old settlements, abandoned villages,
fathers known and unknown, scrambled
evidence, lost tongues.

Dark cat, I stealthily reenter
the country of my origin.
It does not give itself easily.
It hides its fawns. The rainbow
snake sinks its subtle spectrum
in swamps. The scarlet snake and coral
hide their red and yellow bands.
I eat its mushroom visions,
looking for passages in it never unlocked.
It will not learn my name.
My feet feel their way
by a braille my brain cannot read.
I listen, my whole body a tongue.

The Ceremonies

It was our best festival.
Always in high summer,
On Grandpa's birthday, together,
Aunts, uncles, and cousins
Loaded car trunks and trucks
With tools, lunch, ice tea,
And drove to the cemetery
To clean around the graves.
And hearing again who this
Or that one was, we tried

To draw from old folks' minds
A girl our age, who played
With our own mothers, and dead
Brothers and sisters who looked
Like our own baby pictures.

Though cousins married outside,
Our square lot's low curb barred
Some ten acres of dead.
We children strayed toward graves
Of children or revisited
Old dirt mounds without stones,
New graves with wilted flowers,
And always ended at the oldest
Whose concrete top, caved
In, had once arched, but now
Some worn-out dates, a dash,
Broken on the name.

We thought he was our lost
Grandfather, the cavity almost
Hidden by a red cedar
Whose brown needles covered
The bones as the tree and the man
Mixed in one grave with
Rain, this continent and
What we wanted him to be—
Red skin, leathered, wiser,
Not to live or rise
Again but always to be there,
The Indian on the nickel
In our pockets, the one we matched with
And had not yet spent, the father
We dispossessed in the common
Grave of repressed dreams.

Death's dull uniform
Dwarfed obelisks crusted
With marble birds faceless
Angels shepherds woolly
Lambs blur like dulled
Poppies in a distant field

We hurried past, returning
To the motions of living parents—
Her there, kneeling beside
His grave cupping a mound
Of dirt around the flowering
Vine winding the cross stone.
She would raise one knee to rise,
Stop to weed around
The edges, rise, then stoop
To pull a handful of sage
From the hedge. I wondered
If she thought that through
His slab the bonedust knew,
And if he still decayed.

Only the sun's rays
Credible, we cleaned the curb
And fence, raked, cropped
Found a turtle egg the ground
Exposed, gray leather time
Capsule we put on the cool
Meeting house pulpit and forced
In a house without locks
Where no one lived and only
The illicit made love
Then held a somber service
For the fetus of one turtle.
This cradle was his tomb
And though he was not old
He is shrivelled. Brother,
This was our brother; Sister,
Your child. We all hummed
A hymn in the hot afternoon
As we laid it in the sunless ground,
In the turtle's heart, and mine,
Where at times he still turns
Grandpa's beaked but blank face
Toward being, then turns it away.

Bellair

Pait, pieet, pweat, the ivory-bill's
Shrill cry rips through pinewoods;
The charred eye leaps into flame;
The flame-crested head ignites the green needles.
And in the hot months, there
To the open pine-shaded woods would repair
The ladies, small sons, and daughters
Of planters and merchants. All summer long
Mockingbirds, thrashers and warblers
Sheltered in the light green leaves of the redbud and dogwood
Sang of how some late-blooming magnolia,
With its white fleshy flower, or persistent wisteria
Made every fragrance and bloom in the forest despair—
Wild Rose, Pine Sap, Honey-balls, Rose-pink, Mad-dog Skullcap.
    Bellair, Bellair, Bellair,
The war has carried you away with the cotton and slaves,
And the ivory-bill who watched from the highest pine
Swooped down again. *Pieeet, paieet, peet.*

They curtsied and smiled and tried to learn to sing
The formal airs of Italy and the Rhine.
They fled malaria and the dog days for games.
They played out long, innocuous pantomimes,
Half-literate in a wilderness of mosquitoes.
In the scent of the turpentine boxes on the slave-slashed pines,
They fluttered their fans like heavy butterflies
With dwarfed, deformed wings, while servants smiled
And scavenged the bushes to root out rattlesnake nests.
They imagined themselves nymphs in a sylvan glade
Cavorting with gods (fastidious soldiers who got
Wealth and land for killing women and children—
For Jackson, the Butcher). Call their names,
Call—
    Pait, pieet, pieet.

Turner Cassity

Carpenters

Forgiven, unforgiven, they who drive the nails
　　Know what they do: they hammer.
If they doubt, if their vocation fails,
　　They only swell the number,

Large already, of the mutineers and thieves.
　　With only chance and duty
There to cloak them, they elect and nail.
　　The vinegar will pity.

Judas who sops, their silver his accuser, errs
　　To blame the unrewarded.
They guard the branch he hangs from. Guilt occurs
　　Where it can be afforded.

The New Dolores Leather Bar

I adjure thee, respond from thine altars,
　　　　Our Lady of Pain.
　　—A. C. Swinburne

Not quite alone from night to night you'll find them.
Who need so many shackles to remind them
Must doubt that they are prisoners of love.

The leather creaks; studs shine: the chain mail jingles.
Shoulders act as other forms of bangles
In a taste where push has come to shove.

So far from hardhats and so near to Ziegfeld,
They, their costume, fail. Trees felled, each twig felled,
One sees the forest: Redneck Riding Hood's.

Does better-dear-to-eat-you drag, with basket,
Make the question moot? Go on and ask it.
Red, do you deliver, warm, the goods?

Or is the axle-grease, so butch an aura,
Underneath your nails in fact mascara?
Caution, lest your lie, your skin unscarred,

Profane these clanking precincts of the pain queen.
Numb with youth, an amateur procaine queen,
In the rite you lose the passage. Hard,

To know the hurt the knowledge. Command is late now,
Any offer master of your fate now.
You can, though won't, escape. Tarnishing whore,

So cheap your metal and so thin your armor,
Fifteen years will have you once more farmer.
Mammon values; earth and pain ignore.
Name your price and serve him well before.

Fred Chappell

Cleaning the Well

Two worlds there are. One you think
You know; the Other is the Well.
In hard December down I went.
"Now clean it out good." Lord, I sank
Like an anchor. My grand-dad leant
Above. His face blazed bright as steel.

Two worlds, I tell you. Swallowed by stones
Adrip with sweat, I spun on the ache
Of the rope; the pulley shrieked like bones
Scraped merciless on violins.
Plunging an eye. Plunging a lake
Of corkscrew vertigo and silence.

I halfway knew the rope would break.

Two suns I entered. At exact noon,
The white sun narrowly hung above;
Below, like an acid floating moon,
The sun of water shone.
And what beneath that? A monster trove

Of blinding treasure I imagined:
Ribcage of drowned warlock gleaming,
Rust-chewed chain mail, or a plangent
Sunken bell tolling to the heart
Of earth. (They'd surely chosen an art-
less child to sound this soundless dreaming

O.) Dropping like a meteor,
I cried aloud—"Whoo! It's *God*
Damn cold!"—dancing the skin of the star.
"You watch your mouth, young man," he said.
I jerked and cursed in a silver fire
Of cold. My left leg thrummed like a wire.

Then, numb. Well water rose to my waist
And I became a figure of glass,
A naked explorer of outer space.
Felt I'd fricasseed my ass.
Felt I could stalk through earth and stone,
Nerveless creature without a bone.

Water-sun shattered, jelly-
bright wavelets lapped the walls.
Whatever was here to find, I stood
in the lonesome icy belly
Of the darkest vowel, lacking breath and balls,
Brain gummed mud.

"Say, Fred, how's it going down there?"
His words like gunshots roared; re-roared.
I answered, "Well—" (*Well well well . . .*)
And gave it up. It goes like Hell,
I thought. Precise accord
Of pain, disgust, and fear.

"Clean it out good." He drifted pan
And dipper down. I knelt and dredged
The well floor. Ice-razors edged
My eyes, the blackness flamed like fever,
Tin became nerve in my hand
Bodiless. *I shall arise never.*

What did I find under this black sun?
Twelve plastic pearls, monopoly
Money, a greenish rotten cat,
Rubber knife, toy gun,
Clock guts, wish book, door key,
An indescribable female hat.

Was it worth the trip, was it true Descent?
Plumbing my childhood, to fall
Through the hole in the world and become . . .
What? *He told me to go. I went.*
(Recalling something beyond recall.
Cold cock on the nether roof of Home.)

Slouch sun swayed like a drunk
As up he hauled me, up, up,
Most willing fish that was ever caught.
I quivered galvanic in the taut
Loop, wobbled on the solid lip
Of earth, scarcely believing my luck.

His ordinary world too rich
For me, too sudden. Frozen blue,

Dead to armpit, I could not keep
My feet. I shut my eyes to fetch
Back holy dark. Now I knew
All my life uneasy sleep.

Jonah, Joseph, Lazarus,
Were you delivered so? Ript untimely
From black wellspring of death, unseemly
Haste of flesh dragged forth?
Artemis of waters, succor us,
Oversurfeit with our earth.

My vision of light trembled like steam.
I could not think. My senses drowned
In Arctic Ocean, the Pleiades
Streaked in my head like silver fleas.
I could not say what I had found.
I cannot say my dream.

When life began re-tickling my skin
My bones shuddered me. Sun now stood
at one o'clock. Yellow. Thin.
I had not found death good.
"Down there I kept thinking I was dead."

"Aw, you're all right," he said.

My Grandmother Washes Her Feet

I see her still, unsteadily riding the edge
Of the clawfoot tub, mumbling to her feet,
Musing bloodrust water about her ankles.
Cotton skirt pulled up, displaying bony
Bruised patchy calves that would make you weep.

Rinds of her soles had darkened, crust-colored—
Not yellow now—like the tough outer belly
Of an adder. In fourteen hours the most refreshment
She'd given herself was dabbling her feet in the water.

"You mightn't've liked John-Giles. Everybody knew
He was a mean one, galloping whiskey and bad women
All night. Tried to testify dead drunk
In church one time. That was a ruckus. Later
Came back a War Hero, and all the young men
Took to doing the things he did. And failed.
Finally one of his women's men shot him."

"What for?"

       "Stealing milk through fences. . . . That part
Of Family nobody wants to speak of.
They'd rather talk about fine men, brick houses,
Money. Maybe you ought to know, teach you
Something."

       "What *do* they talk about?"

              "Generals,
And the damn Civil War, and marriages.
Things you brag about in the front of Bibles.
You'd think there was arms and legs of Family
On every battlefield from Chickamauga
to Atlanta."

       "That's not the way it is?"

"Don't matter how it is. No proper way
To talk, is all. It was nothing they ever did.
And plenty they *won't* talk about . . . John-Giles!"

Her cracked toes thumped the tub wall, spreading
Shocklets. Amber toenails curled like shavings.
She twisted the worn knob to pour in coolness
I felt suffuse her body like a whiskey.

"Bubba Martin, he was another, and no
Kind of man. Jackleg preacher with the brains
Of a toad. Read the Bible upsidedown and crazy
Till it drove him crazy, making crazy marks
On doorsills, windows, sides of Luther's barn.
He killed hisself at last with a shotgun.
No gratitude for Luther putting him up
All those years. Shot so he'd fall down the well."

"I never heard."

"They never mention him.
Nor Aunt Annie, that everybody called
Paregoric Annie, that roamed the highways
Thumbing cars and begging change to keep
Even with her craving. She claimed she was saving up
To buy a glass eye. It finally shamed them
Enough, they went together and got her one.
That didn't stop her. She lugged it around
In a velvet-lined case, asking strangers
Please to drop it in the socket for her.
They had her put away. And that was that.
There's places Family ties just won't stretch to."

Born then in my mind a race of beings
Unknown and monstrous. I named them Shadow-Cousins,
A linked long dark line of them,
Peering from mirrors and gleaming in closets, agog
To manifest themselves inside myself.
Like discovering a father's cancer.
I wanted to search my body for telltale streaks.

"Sounds like a bunch of cow thieves."

"Those too, I reckon,
But they're forgotten or covered over so well
Not even I can make them out. Gets foggy
When folks decide they're coming on respectable.
First thing you know, you'll have a Family Tree."

(I imagined a wind-stunted horse-apple.)

She raised her face. The moons of the naked bulb
Flared in her spectacles, painting out her eyes.
In dirty water light bobbed like round soap.
A countenance matter-of-fact, age-engraved,
Mulling in peaceful wonder petty annals
Of embarrassment. Gray but edged with brown
Like an old photograph, her hair shone yellow.
A tiredness mantled her fine energy.
She shifted, sluicing water under instep.

"O what's the use," she said. "Water seeks
Its level. If your daddy thinks that teaching school
In a white shirt makes him a likelier man,
What's to blame? Leastways, he won't smother
Of mule-farts or have to starve for a pinch of rainfall.
Nothing new gets started without the old's
Plowed under, or halfway under. We sprouted from dirt,
Though, and it's with you, and dirt you'll never forget."

"No Mam."

      "Don't you say me No Mam yet.
Wait till you get your chance to deny it."

Once she giggled, a sound like stroking muslin.

"You're bookish. I can see you easy a lawyer
Or a county clerk in a big white suit and tie,
Feeding the preacher and bribing the sheriff and the judge.
Second-generation-respectable
Don't come to any better destiny.
But it's dirt you rose from, dirt you'll bury in.
Just about the time you'll think your blood
Is clean, here will come dirt in a natural shape
You never dreamed. It'll rise up saying, Fred,
Where's that mule you're supposed to march behind?
Where's your overalls and roll-your-owns?
Where's your Blue Tick hounds and Domineckers?
Not all the money in the world can wash true-poor
True rich. Fatback just won't change to artichokes."

"What's artichokes?"

      "Pray Jesus you'll never know.
For if you do it'll be a sign you've grown
Away from what you are, can fly to flinders
Like a touch-me-not . . . I may have errored
When I said *true-poor*. It ain't the same
As dirt-poor. When you got true dirt you got
Everything you need . . . And don't you say me
Yes Mam again. You just wait."

      She leaned
and pulled the plug. The water circled gagging

To a bloody eye and poured in the hole like a rat.
I thought maybe their spirits had gathered there,
All my Shadow-Cousins clouding the water,
And now they ran to earth and would cloud the earth.
Effigies of soil, I could seek them out
By clasping soil, forcing warm rude fingers
Into ancestral jelly my father wouldn't plow.
I strained to follow them, and never did.
I never had the grit to stir those guts.
I never had the guts to stir that earth.

February

Wouldn't drive and wouldn't be led,
So they tied cotton line around its neck and it backed,
Clipped steps, as the rope stretched.
Whereat,
They shot it clean through the shrieking brain.
And it dropped in a lump.

                The boy, dismayed
With delight, watches the hog-killing,
Sharply alive in its tangle. Recoils,
Tries to hold it sensible; fails;
All the meaning in a brutal hour.

They bring the sledge down, and difficult
With the horse plunging white-eyed, hoofs
Askitter in the slick steep bank; the blood-smell's
Frightful and he snorts, head clatters back.
The pig's still gently quivering,
                he's got a blue and human eye.
Lug it over and tumble it on, and the horse
Goes straining. The men swear
And grin, their teeth show hard in piercing air.

            Frost gauzy on leaf and stone,
            The sky but faintly blue, wiped white.

. . .And into the yard. The fire popping and licking,
They roll the big black cauldron to it. Saturday,
The neighbor women and men and kids, the faces
Broad with excitement. Wow wow across the gravel,
The cast iron pot; settles on the flame,
Black egg in its scarlet nest. Dark speech of the men,
Women waiting silent, hands under the blue aprons.

Long spike rammed through the heels
And up he goes against the big-armed oak
And dipped down in, dipped again, so
His hair falls off. (Swims in the filmed water
Like giant eyelashes.) Like a silver gourd
His belly shines and bulges. He's opened
And his steam goes up white,
The ghost of hog in the glassy morning.
They catch his guts.

                      The child, elated-drunk
With the horror, as they undo joint
And joint, stands with the men, watches
Their arms. They yank and slash, stammer
Of blood on the denim, eyelets of blood
On arm and fabric. They laugh like scythes,
Setting the head aside to see the dismantling
With its own blue eyes—still smiles
A thin smug smile!

              And they cleave it
And cleave it. Loins. Ham.
                Shoulder. Feet. Chops.
Even the tail's an obscure prize.
Goes into buckets; the child hauls
From hand to hand the pail all dripping.
Top of the heap, tremulous as water, lies
The big maroon liver.

              And the women receive it.
Gravely waiting as for supper grace.

The kitchen is glossy with heat, surcharged
With the smell of hog. Every surface

Is raddled with the fat. He slides
His finger on the jamb, it feels like flesh.
The whole lower house juicy with hog,
A bit of it in every cranny.
Where does it all come from?
                (A most unlikely prodigious pig.)
And now the women, busy, talk
Within the great clouds of oil and steam, bared
Elbows, heads nodding like breezy jonquils.
Clash of kettles, spoons
Yammering in the bowls, the windows opaque gray
With pig.

The sun reaches under the tree. They're gleaning
The last of him and the slippery whiskey jar
Goes handily among them. Wipe their mouths
With greasy wrists. And the smug head
Burst and its offerings distributed. Brain.
Ears. And the tail handed off with a clap of laughter.
They lick the white whiskey and laugh.

And his bladder and his stomach sack! puffed
Up and tied off and flung to the kids,
Game balls, they bat them about,
Running full tilt head down across the scattered yard.
And then on a startled breeze
The bladder's hoist, vaults high and gleams in the sunlight
And reflects on its shiny globe
The sky a white square
And the figures beneath, earnest figures
Gazing straight up.

John William Corrington

For a Woodscolt Miscarried

I know the barn where they got you
the night they tricked each other
and themselves.

In that season, the nights are
full of rain, the sky shakes
like a lost child and for an hour
it is cool enough to love.

Out of such cool love you came
to burgeon day by day,
carelessly made and moving darkly
like the land your most distant bending
fathers tilled, crying for Israel,
hoping for Jesus.

Your nearly mother felt trouble in her depths
where an ignorant angel stirred the waters
with his holy staff.
She sat big on the shack's long porch
watching cars dart South for Baton Rouge,
watching fingers of young pine fondle
tumid clouds above the field and shed
where you took place.

Cars throbbed toward the city. The shack
stayed where it was. And stayed
till her time came. And yours.

At the clinic they found something wrong;
her blood, his seed—your own blind weaving
of them both. They said that you were dead.
And it was so.

Some time in the sixth month you gave it up.
Maybe you heard some talk of what there was,
could feel the chill dissension in her gut:
her wanting and her fearing and her shame.
And gave it up. Collapsed, began to junk
limbs and fingers,
the tassel of your kind,

the piggish brooding something like a face.
Each cell dissolved, left off its yearning,
its moist prophecies.

In the Felicianas,
there are no coffins for what is not born
but loosed, a stewy discharge almost the same
as if the bowels went wrong.
Preachers, fine at birth, adroit at marriage,
inured to burial,
have no rite for those who almost were.
A near thing does not count.
A miss had just as well be fifty miles.

Just as well: no matter what they say
each coming and each leaving is a feast,
a celebration of the sun we squall to see
and weep to leave: a leaping forth,
a going down, each swings its own harsh joy
and the round of its perfection has no words.
But for you, what?
Who lay for a brief time within
the confines of her deep uneasy space,
your sun her heart thundering there above
red as the wounds of Jesus.
Who turned and turned amidst a tideless
inward sea as ghosts of her body
taught your spindrift hands to be
and made a tongue for speech and eyes to see.

For you, what?

Somewhere near in the fields your father
turns the land waiting for a first
bold thrust of green out of the earth's
confusion. Maybe relieved, as mute and
unaware as she, he will watch the stalks
and leaves spread out, will bless
the flower and the bole. Will shout and
carry the first opened fruit,
a pale victory, running down the rows
pulling its long staple through his fingers
like a sheaf of dollar bills.

And you who lost nothing that you had,
no trees or blooms or words
rising against Louisiana's sun, will stir,
if ever, in the evening breeze, a trouble missed,
a junction passed and never seen
like a field or shack at the edge of sight
down a highway to the Gulf.

pastoral

in the fields
         where larks emoted
         where tender summer
      groomed green children
and the miraculous
           sea wove its
      breath among parvenu leaves

tiny cattle strolled in the
      circle of a wooden bell
      demi-sheep cropped wonderful
           vegetables
      along a stream wound silver
         through rare trees

—my god, farmer surakawa gasped
      the breath of armageddon
         on his neck
           and turned to see
    a brook leap into steam
    cattle tumble
      their delicate legs snapped
      like hoofed matchsticks
    leaves puff white to sift
      on fields of glass
      as larks burst into flame

and on the august horizon
      the city being eaten by a sun

63

lines to the south

ON SEEING AN EQUESTRIAN STATUE OF THE LATE GENL. W. T. SHERMAN

up on his pedestal
the general hunches
stony
    alone
        fulfilled
the dust of old victories
powdering his eyes

a century of loyal pigeons
have honored him
and twined a lime
corona round his head

united rains
collective winds
and central suns
have bleached the
fire and blood
        leaving
a brassy glare
for kids and nurses
confederate against him
frowning back without
a twinge
    and
lovers strolling past
in twilight delirium
echoing his castiron dream
      humming
  georgia on my mind

and under him the swart
pony
    with tarnished teeth
who saw enough near macon
to make a burro cringe
    whose shoulders
      withers
      flanks

shrink from their burden
ooze metallic shame
    whose blind sculptured eyes
look southward with
brute sympathy—

if shermans horse can take it
so can you

Rosemary Daniell

Of Jayne Mansfield, Flannery O'Connor, My Mother & Me
FOR ALICE WALKER, WHOSE BLACKNESS MADE THE ENEMY VISIBLE

Milledgeville, the original capital of Georgia, is known for its azalea-lined streets and its white-columned mansions. The town is also the reluctant site of the state mental institution and the state correctional facility for women.

Myth of the Spanish moss:
within each hard tree a bound
woman writhes: her hair twists
of ash claws crawls the air . . .
in Milledgeville live oaks
blanch the Blood of the Lambs—
debs in white cotton panties
crimped matrons in slips of white
lace all the permanent Daughters
of the Confederacy caught
in their corsets of white
brocade. Yes this is an ash
blonde town the white satin
undergarments of the Baptist
belt of swamps where white
crewcut sheriffs run down blacks
& women. It's three a.m.

& I lie in the John Milledge
Motel room 4D where Jayne
Mansfield slept a half mile
down highway 441
from the white town house where
Flannery stitched the white
home ec apron required for her
graduation from the same
school where my mother wore
white middy blouses wrote on
white notebook paper "I want
to marry a lawyer live in
a house with white columns. . . ."

& trying not to hear through
white walls the sounds of white

male cursing I think Jayne
her white satin hair spreading
her white plastic breasts rising
beneath this cover of white
chenille the white white sperm
of half of Amerika gliding
across her light pancaked cheeks—
& imagine Flannery sweet
between her white girl's sheets
watching upon a white white
ceiling blank white pages
the petit fours with white icing
of literary teas & now flash
my mother her Pond's palms
pressed against her magnolia
petal face dreaming the blond
man who would save her the white
white roses the white satin
wedding the honeymoon trip.

Yet listening to the *mother
fuckers sons of bitches*
the brute motel plans made by
white southern men I wonder:
did Jayne see already her
decapitation on a dark road
outside New Orleans her head
that Clairol-pale egg severed
as in life from her body?
Or did Flannery Catholic &
weird feel even then the wolf
disease eating out her teen-
age limbs: the falling hair
melting hipbones the hospital
cuff tightening tightening?

& did my mother even before
my Cherokee tinged father—
the drinking & the gambling—
the bills & torn underwear—
sob into her dormitory
pillow bubbling within her

belle's brainpain with the
lobotomies of marriage
the electrodes for shock her
suicide at sixty? Yes

did each of them: Jayne
her throat neatly stitched
Flannery her face turned
moony by cortisone my mother
whitened to wax by Revlon
her upper lip bleached blonde
wearing her best white gold
costume jewelry yes did
each of them know lying
in this white satin lined
sarcophagus for women that
the first drop of blood ruins
the crotches of white cotton
panties spots the slips of
white nylon lace stains the backs
of white wedding dresses yes
turns each of us scarlet women
deserving of mutilation
disease damnation that we
like the women in the trees
are embalmed & recalling
my rage washing between pale
blue lines the blood-black scrawl
of my mother's girlish plans
I wonder what sleep awaits me—
freak of cunt & brain in this
place pure white chaste that
murders women murders women.

Ann Deagon

Moving North

The Brown Recluse, also known as the Hermit Fiddler, a spider whose bite produces a gangrenous sore, is apparently spreading northward. From its original home in the Southwest it has now migrated as far as North Carolina.

Not it. She. The one with eggs.
Demographer with the future in her belly,
moving up in the world. Texas rots
dry, Louisiana wet. Twenty
years in Alabama: closets, drawers,
silver chests, the backs of portraits
cottoned with eggs and everywhere the sweet
festering scent. In Tennessee
she homed into the woodpile, roughed it,
budded the boards with eggs. Now here
holed up in my ornamental block
she babysits a quiet contagion.

         Lady,
I know your bite. I am myself
something of a recluse and given
to wearing brown. My Odyssey—
no, my Penelopeid up the dry
shins of girlhood to the wetter parts
was not unlike your own. We are heading
both of us north. The cold, I hear,
is shriveling, the cold bites back.
Even in this lush midway state I feel
a touch of gangrene on my hither leg,
some deadlier hermit fiddling in my brain.

Basic Rescue

1. Open the Airway

Green cement has flooded the firehall.
We unfold chairs. The instructor
lays flat a white sheet.

He inflates Resusci-Anne,
pumps till her bent legs kick straight.
LOOK LISTEN AND FEEL FOR BREATHING.
She does not breathe. GIVE FOUR
QUICK BREATHS. We kneel and breathe
turn by turn in a discreet pavane
each of us with her own death in tow.

2. Feel for a Pulse

Each of us with her own death in tow:
the baby turned blue in its highchair
the boy at the bottom of the pool
like a mosaic, the daughter O.D.'d
the man in the bed now waking up.

We crouch, fingertips to carotid
feeling for pulse we know's not there.
All the world has a single throat.

3. Begin Compression

All the world has a single throat.
See how she lolls, lips parted, knowing
she is born to this, hers to invite
the mouths of strangers. She inhales us
not tasting our garlic or our mouthwash
tasting only our pale clear lives.

The heel of our hand is between her breasts.
We are pumping up the world, see how
its vasty chambers fill. We will breathe
life into the mouths of corpses:
their lungs redden like a forge.

Going Under

I

Ellen enters the pool:
eleven, breastless she breasts the water
her sutured heart powerful as surf
(below her nipple the red cicatrice
remembers intensive care).
Splashes close her eyes, she shouts
    Marco . . .
the writhing children plunge,
scatter, their round mouths answer
    Polo . . . Polo . . .
She launches blind
through the liquid sounds
catching at her childhood.

II

Face down on this glass-bottomed bed I map
sunken Venice, luminous through
layered aquamarine. The girl
Elena enters the church of San Marco:
maidens swirl about her, pearls
entwine her emerald hair.
Inside the nave phosphorescent as
a sea-cave candles waver, the round
notes of choirboys surface like bubbles.
Nicolo Polo takes his bride.
She will name their son Marco.

III

And he was like a god
who entered you, got you with child,
cast off for Constantinople, visited
the court of the Grand Khan, and like
Odysseus lingered twenty years?
Penelope had choices. Yours dissolved
in that first rending childbirth when
the flesh canal ran water, blood, and your
fresh life into the brackish grave.

Venice, where every burial is
a putting to sea.

IV

Face up in the embrace of stone you age.
Brine condenses on your lashes like
crystalline coronals, your eyes awash
inside the liquifying skull; your skin
paler than beauty wrinkles in the saline
secrecy of the vault.

                Marco full grown
greets his father at the wharf. Of all
his merchantry the fairest bargain this,
and most Venetian: a woman for a son.
Not the doge only
marries the sea.

V

Ellen, Elena, sisters, we are wed
to an interior and bloody sea.
We take its tides to realms exotic as
Marco's extravagances, hazard there
our damask bodies.
                Ellen, daughter,
the scalpel has made you perfect, arch your
perfect body downward, plunge past
heraldic Venice wreathed in tentacles,
sea-caves and mermen, past the glimmering past,
lower than color, luminescence, tide—
where in dark-standing deep
egg-laden hulks
celebrate their soundless nuptials.

James Dickey

Cherrylog Road

Off Highway 106
At Cherrylog Road I entered
The '34 Ford without wheels,
Smothered in kudzu,
With a seat pulled out to run
Corn whiskey down from the hills.

And then from the other side
Crept into an Essex
With a rumble seat of red leather
And then out again, aboard
A blue Chevrolet, releasing
The rust from its other color,

Reared up on three building blocks.
None had the same body heat;
I changed with them inward, toward
The weedy heart of the junkyard,
For I knew that Doris Holbrook
Would escape from her father at noon

And would come from the farm
To seek parts owned by the sun
Among the abandoned chassis,
Sitting in each in turn
As I did, leaning forward
As in a wild stock-car race

In the parking lot of the dead.
Time after time, I climbed in
And out the other side, like
An envoy or movie star
Met at the station by crickets.
A radiator cap raised its head,

Become a real toad or a kingsnake
As I neared the hub of the yard,
Passing through many states,
Many lives, to reach
Some grandmother's long Pierce-Arrow
Sending platters of blindness forth

From its nickel hubcaps
And spilling its tender upholstery
On sleepy roaches,
The glass panel in between
Lady and colored driver
Not all the way broken out,

The back-seat phone
Still on its hook.
I got in as though to exclaim,
"Let us go to the orphan asylum,
John: I have some old toys
For children who say their prayers."

I popped with sweat as I thought
I heard Doris Holbrook scrape
Like a mouse in the southern-state sun
That was eating the paint in blisters
From a hundred car tops and hoods.
She was tapping like code,

Loosening the screws,
Carrying off headlights,
Sparkplugs, bumpers,
Cracked mirrors and gear-knobs,
Getting ready, already,
To go back with something to show

Other than her lips' new trembling
I would hold to me soon, soon,
Where I sat in the ripped back seat
Talking over the interphone,
Praying for Doris Holbrook
To come from her father's farm

And to get back there
With no trace of me on her face
To be seen by her red-haired father
Who would change, in the squalling barn,
Her back's pale skin with a strop,
Then lay for me

In a bootlegger's roasting car
with a string-triggered 12-gauge shotgun

To blast the breath from the air.
Not cut by the jagged windshields,
Through the acres of wrecks she came
With a wrench in her hand,

Through dust where the blacksnake dies
Of boredom, and the beetle knows
The compost has no more life.
Someone outside would have seen
The oldest car's door inexplicably
Close from within:

I held her and held her and held her,
Convoyed at terrific speed
By the stalled, dreaming traffic around us,
So the blacksnake, stiff
With inaction, curved back
Into life, and hunted the mouse

With deadly overexcitement,
The beetles reclaimed their field
As we clung, glued together,
With the hooks of the seat springs
Working through to catch us red-handed
Amidst the gray, breathless batting

That burst from the seat at our backs.
We left by separate doors
Into the changed, other bodies
Of cars, she down Cherrylog Road
And I to my motorcycle
Parked like the soul of the junkyard

Restored, a bicycle fleshed
With power, and tore off
Up Highway 106, continually
Drunk on the wind in my mouth,
Wringing the handlebar for speed,
Wild to be wreckage forever.

The Heaven of Animals

Here they are. The soft eyes open.
If they have lived in a wood
It is a wood.
If they have lived on plains
It is grass rolling
Under their feet forever.

Having no souls, they have come,
Anyway, beyond their knowing.
Their instincts wholly bloom
And they rise.
The soft eyes open.

To match them, the landscape flowers,
Outdoing, desperately
Outdoing what is required:
The richest wood,
The deepest field.

For some of these,
It could not be the place
It is, without blood.
These hunt, as they have done,
But with claws and teeth grown perfect,

More deadly than they can believe.
They stalk more silently,
And crouch on the limbs of trees,
And their descent
Upon the bright backs of their prey

May take years
In a sovereign floating of joy.
And those that are hunted
Know this as their life,
Their reward: to walk

Under such trees in full knowledge
Of what is in glory above them,
And to feel no fear,
But acceptance, compliance.
Fulfilling themselves without pain

At the cycle's center,
They tremble, they walk
Under the tree,
They fall, they are torn,
They rise, they walk again.

The Performance

The last time I saw Donald Armstrong
He was staggering oddly off into the sun,
Going down, of the Philippine Islands.
I let my shovel fall, and put that hand
Above my eyes, and moved some way to one side
That his body might pass through the sun,

And I saw how well he was not
Standing there on his hands,
On his spindle-shanked forearms balanced,
Unbalanced, with his big feet looming and waving
In the great, untrustworthy air
He flew in each night, when it darkened.

Dust fanned in scraped puffs from the earth
Between his arms, and blood turned his face inside out,
To demonstrate its suppleness
Of veins, as he perfected his role.
Next day, he toppled his head off
On an island beach to the south,

And the enemy's two-handed sword
Did not fall from anyone's hands
At that miraculous sight,
As the head rolled over upon
Its wide-eyed face, and fell
Into the inadequate grave

He had dug for himself, under pressure.
Yet I put my flat hand to my eyebrows
Months later, to see him again
In the sun, when I learned how he died,

And imagined him, there,
Come, judged, before his small captors,

Doing all his lean tricks to amaze them—
The back somersault, the kip-up—
And at last, the stand on his hands,
Perfect, with his feet together,
His head down, evenly breathing,
As the sun poured up from the sea

And the headsman broke down
In a blaze of tears, in that light
Of the thin, long human frame
Upside down in its own strange joy,
And, if some other one had not told him,
Would have cut off the feet

Instead of the head,
And if Armstrong had not presently risen
In kingly, round-shouldered attendance,
And then knelt down in himself
Beside his hacked, glittering grave, having done
All things in his life that he could.

Adultery

We have all been in rooms
We cannot die in, and they are odd places, and sad.
Often Indians are standing eagle-armed on hills

In the sunrise   open wide to the Great Spirit
Or gliding in canoes   or cattle are browsing on the walls
Far away   gazing down with the eyes of our children

Not far away   or there are men driving
The last railspike, which has turned
Gold in their hands. Gigantic forepleasure lives

Among such scenes, and we are alone with it
At last. There is always some weeping
Between us   and someone is always checking

A wrist watch by the bed to see how much
Longer we have left. Nothing can come
Of this   nothing can come

Of us: of me with my grim techniques
Or you who have sealed your womb
With a ring of convulsive rubber:

Although we come together,
Nothing will come of us. But we would not give
It up, for death is beaten

By praying Indians   by distant cows   historical
Hammers   by hazardous meetings that bridge
A continent. One could never die here

Never die   never die
While crying. My lover, my dear one
I will see you next week

When I'm in town. I will call you
If I can. Please get hold of   please don't
Oh God, Please don't any more I can't bear . . . Listen:

We have done it again   we are
Still living. Sit up and smile,
God bless you. Guilt is magical.

The Shark's Parlor

Memory: I can take my head and strike it on a wall   on Cumberland
     Island
Where the night tide came crawling under the stairs   came up the first
Two or three steps   and the cottage stood on poles all night
With the sea sprawled under it   as we dreamed of the great fin circling
Under the bedroom floor.   In daylight there was my first brassy taste of
     beer
And Payton Ford and I came back from the Glynn County slaughter-
     house
With a bucket of entrails and blood. We tied one end of a hawser
To a spindling porch pillar and rowed straight out of the house

Three hundred yards into the vast front yard of windless blue water
The rope outslithering its coil   the two-gallon jug stoppered and sealed
With wax   and a ten-foot chain leader   a drop-forged shark hook
     nestling.
We cast our blood on the waters   the land blood easily passing
For sea blood   and we sat in it for a moment with the stain
     spreading
Out from the boat   sat in a new radiance   in the pond of blood in the
     sea
Waiting for fins   waiting to spill our guts also in the glowing water.
We dumped the bucket, and baited the hook with a run-over collie pup.
     The jug
Bobbed, trying to shake off the sun as a dog would shake off the sea.
We rowed to the house   feeling the same water lift the boat a new way,
All the time seeing where we lived rise and dip with the oars.
We tied up and sat down in rocking chairs, one eye or the other
     responding
To the blue-eye wink of the jug. Payton got us a beer and we sat

All morning sat there with blood on our minds   the red mark out
In the harbor slowly failing us   then   the house groaned   the rope
Sprang out of the water   splinters flew   we leapt from our chairs
And grabbed the rope   hauled   did nothing   the house coming
     subtly
Apart   all around us   underfoot   boards beginning to sparkle like
     sand
With the glinting of the bright hidden parts of ten-year-old nails
Pulling out   the tarred poles we slept propped-up on   leaning to sea
As in land wind   crabs scuttling from under the floor   as we took
     turns about
Two more porch pillars   and looked out and saw   something   a
     fish-flash
An almighty fin in trouble   a moiling of secret forces   a false start
Of water   a round wave growing: in the whole of Cumberland Sound
     the one ripple.
Payton took off without a word   I could not hold him either

But clung to the rope anyway: it was the whole house bending
Its nails that held whatever it was   coming in a little and like a fool
I took up the slack on my wrist. The rope drew gently   jerked   I
     lifted
Clean off the porch and hit the water   the same water it was in

80

I felt in blue blazing terror at the bottom of the stairs and scrambled
Back up looking desperately into the human house as deeply as I could
Stopping my gaze before it went out the wire screen of the back door
Stopped it on the thistled rattan   the rugs I lay on and read
On my mother's sewing basket with next winter's socks spilling from it
The flimsy vacation furniture   a bucktoothed picture of myself.
Payton came back with three men from a filling station   and glanced at
    me
Dripping water   inexplicable   then we all grabbed hold like a tug-
    of-war.

We were gaining a little   from us a cry went up   from everywhere
People came running. Behind us the house filled with men and boys.
On the third step from the sea I took my place   looking down the rope
Going into the ocean, humming and shaking off drops. A houseful
Of people put their backs into it   going up the steps from me
Into the living room   through the kitchen   down the back stairs
Up and over a hill of sand   across a dust road   and onto a raised field
Of dunes   we were gaining   the rope in my hands began to be wet
With deeper water   all other haulers retreated through the house
But Payton and I on the stairs   drawing hand over hand on our blood
Drawing into existence by the nose   a huge body   becoming
A hammerhead   rolling in beery shallows   and I began to let up
But the rope still strained behind me   the town had gone
Pulling-mad in our house: far away in a field of sand they struggled
They had turned their backs on the sea   bent double   some on their
    knees
The rope over their shoulders like a bag of gold   they strove for the
    ideal
Esso station across the scorched meadow   with the distant fish coming
    up
The front stairs   the sagging boards   still coming in   up   taking
Another step   toward the empty house   where the rope stood
    straining
By itself through the rooms   in the middle of the air. "Pass the word,"
Payton said, and I screamed it: "Let up, good God, let up!" to no one
    there.
The shark flopped on the porch, grating with salt-sand   driving
    back in
The nails he had pulled out   coughing chunks of his formless blood.
The screen door banged and tore off   he scrambled on his tail   slid

Curved   did a thing from another world   and was out of his element
    and in
Our vacation paradise   cutting all four legs from under the dinner table
With one deep-water move   he unwove the rugs in a moment
    throwing pints
Of blood over everything we owned   knocked the buck teeth out of my
    picture
His odd head full of crushed jelly-glass splinters and radio tubes
    thrashing
Among the pages of fan magazines   all the movie stars drenched in
    sea-blood.
Each time we thought he was dead   he struggled back and smashed
One more thing   in all coming back to die   three or four more times
    after death.
At last we got him out   log-rolling him   greasing his sandpaper
    skin
With lard to slide him   pulling on his chained lips as the tide came
Tumbled him down the steps as the first night wave went under the floor.
He drifted off   head back   belly white as the moon. What could I do
    but buy
That house   for the one black mark still there   against death   a
    forehead-
toucher in the room he circles beneath   and has been invited to wreck?
Blood hard as iron on the wall   black with time   still bloodlike
Can be touched whenever the brow is drunk enough: all changes:
    Memory:
Something like three-dimensional dancing in the limbs   with age
Feeling more in two worlds than one   in all worlds the growing
    encounters.

R. H. W. Dillard

Kite

FOR JUDY

A kite holds in the April air
So steady a crossbow's bolt
Could trace the string
Straight to its crossed sticks.

You approve what Hammett
Said, that things belong
To those who want them most.

The kite climbs and hovers
In the steady air like a kite,
One of the "hawks of southern
Distribution," shaped like a falcon,
Wings sharp as the bolt of a crossbow,
Flat as a magpie in the April sky.

You are focussed in the steady light
So sharply the day centers on you.
The kite string unwinds like film.
The bright sun clicks like a shutter.

The kite opens like a light sail
In a light wind, bounces once
Like a note, crosses
The sun like a wink.

The day belongs to you to give
Or save. The kite steadies
The April air. The sun centers
Like a kite across the day,
Like the sharp pupil in the iris
Of the sky, blue as the focus
Of an open eye.

Charles Edward Eaton

The Nude Poet

All of the mattresses worn through, he lies
On a bed of stone, the ironic pea
The tense princess kept doubling in her mind.
All one had to do was live through the layers
To find that the nerves seldom entirely lie,
A wilderness of stone beneath sensation
As though in every lush feeling a pit
Fell into a quilted effect below.

Nevertheless, the body hoards its memories,
Jacking itself above the bedrock world,
Excreting its fantasies of roses,
Clinging to the splitting hammocks, loose slings—
One feels a single stone a long way off:
There is a piercing stalagmite in love;
Unknown defeat rumbles down, in under;
Death contributes the gravel from a craw.

The nude poet considers his attritions
As if the world, reviewed, stacked bodies up,
Lamina on lamina of lovers,
And the poet himself lies like the felt stone—
So this was the secret of mattresses:
The princess was no liar and no shill.
She is beside him on the bed of stones—
Thick life above them cannot hear their words.

Squashes

Like beheaded geese plucked to their yellow skin they lie in the shade
Of an obscene but stalwart little forest of thick leaves,
Lost in all that heat, in a world they never made.

Brought into the house they lose their murdered, meat-shop look—
I place them along the stone wall on the porch,
Their necks entwined like abstracts of little yellow mandolins
    accompanied by a book.

In a manner of speaking I have arranged for their rescue—
They are handsome as a Braque, accented by that important,
Lyric-looking volume with the jacket of dark blue.

Always and always the suspicion mounts
As we accumulate our world around us and see it rot
That, given the given, it is what we do with a thing that counts.

Which is not to say that now or ever one will quite be done
With whatever dreams itself to be in us at first glance,
Little glutted, yellow-bellied, murdered geese lying in the sun.

But if on closer look the mandolins are warted, not quite so sleekly gold,
And the wind shallows through the pages of the book,
We shall have made our passions for a little while do as they are told.

George Garrett

For a Bitter Season

The oak tree in my front yard dies,
whose leaves are sadder than cheap wrapping paper,
and nothing I can do will keep it long.

Last spring in another place a pear tree
glistened in bloom like a graceful drift of snow.
Birds and bees loved that spacious white

and a daughter was born in the time of flowers.

Now I am a stranger and my oak tree dies
young. Blight without a name, a bad omen.
I die, too, fret in my familiar flesh,

and I take this for a bitter season.
We have lived too long with fear. We take
fear for granted like a drunken uncle,

like a cousin not quite all there
who's always there. I have lived too long
with the stranger who haunts my mirror.

Night in the city and the sirens scream
fresh disasters for my morning paper.
The oak tree in the front yard dies.

Bless us, a houseful of loving strangers,
one good woman, two small boys, a man
waking from sleep to cough his name.

And bless my daughter made of snow and bluest eyes.

Abraham's Knife

Where hills are hard and bare,
rocks like thrown dice, heat
and glare that's clean and pitiless,
a shadow dogs my heels, limp
as a drowned man washed ashore.
True sacrifice is secret, none

to applaud the ceremony, nor
witness to be moved to tears.
No one to see. God alone
knows, Whose great eye winks not,
from Whom no secrets are hid.

My father, I have loved you,
love you now, dead twenty years.
Your ghost shadows me home.
Your laughter and your anger still
trouble my scarecrow head like wings.
My own children, sons and daughter,
study my stranger's face. Their flesh,
bones frail as a small bird's,
is strange, too, in my hands.
What will become of us?
I read my murder in their eyes.

And you, old father, Abraham,
my judge and executioner, I pray
bear witness for me now. I ask
a measure of your faith. Forgive
us, Jew and Gentile, all
your children, all your victims.
In the naked country of no shadow
you raise your hand in shining arc.
And we are fountains of foolish tears
to flood and green the world again.
Strike for my heart. Your blade is light.

Revival

Now chaos has pitched a tent
in my pasture, a circus tent
like a huge toadstool
in the land of giants. Oh,
all night long the voices of
the damned and saved keep me
awake and, *basso*, the evangelist.

Fire and brimstone, thunder and lightning,
telegrams in the unknown tongue!
The bushes are crawling with couples.
I see one girl so leafy that
she might be Daphne herself.

I know there were giants once,
one-eyed wonders of the morning
world. Ponderous, they rode
dinosaurs like Shetland ponies,
timber for toothpicks, boulders for
baseballs, oceans for bathtubs,
whales for goldfish, Great God,
when they shook fists and roared,
stars fell down like snowflakes
under glass! Came then Christ
to climb the thorny beanstalk
and save us one and all.

ARE YOU SAVED?????

Rocks are painted, trees nailed
with signs, fences trampled.
Under the dome of the tent
falls salt of sweat and tears
enough to kill my grass at the roots.
Morning and I'll wake to find
the whole thing gone. Bright dew
and blessed silence. Nothing
to prove they camped here and tried
to raise a crop of hell except
that scar of dead space (where the tent was)
like a huge footprint.

Solitaire

The days shuffle together.
Cards again? No, no, I mean
like convicts in lockstep,

like the patients on the Senile Ward
I saw once, gray and feeble,
blank-eyed creatures in cheap cotton,
pumped full of tranquilizers,
("It's really the efficient way to handle
the situation," an attendant told me.)
so lethargic they could hardly pick up their feet.

The gray days shuffle together.
The trees are picked and plucked,
sad tough fowl not fit for stewing.
The round world is shaved and hairless
like the man in the moon. Screams,
but I can't hear it. Next door
the dog howls and I can.
Break out a fresh deck for God's sake!
Bright kings and queens and one-eyed jacks.
Free prisoners. And let the old men go home.

York Harbor Morning

Where clear air blew off the land
wind turns around and the sky changes.
Where there was burning blue is pale gray now
heavy with the salt and scent of open sea
and the lazy groaning of the foghorn
saying change   change   change
like a sleeper dreaming and breathing.

Tide turning, too, with the weather,
and the lobsterboats swing around to pull
against moorings like large dogs on chains.
Gulls cry like hurt children and vanish,
and I begin to think it was a magician,
bitter and clever, who played this trick.

That old magician is laughing in the fog.
The cries of wounded children fade away

while the bellbuoy rings farewell   farewell
daring the dead to rise from their dreaming
and hold their lives like water in their hands.

Andrew Glaze

My South

I

Before me, it was grandpa's old mad South,
the funhouse of principle.
A sort of Baptist revival in a whorehouse,
with violent rapes in the purities,
and John Locke snatching up the souls
and boiling them down into Presbyterian whisky.

We were so alone with our familyness—
(grandma standing by the cistern threatening to jump in)
and a deep, still, limestone-well of love and service in our dream.
(Grandpa letting out all his money
in personal notes
because he believed in gentlemanliness—
raising a houseful of children
without speaking to his wife.)
We were incessantly and purposely pursuing
any policy that hid our fundamental nature from us.
(Sin is being forced to notice
what you're thinking about all the time anyway.)

What we saw most clearly
wasn't real at all.
In the name of some imaginary world
my Uncle Mike in Florida was shooting at the neighbors,
pursuing property rights like the true cross,
and Aunt Billie stayed at home in Tennessee
to mind the rats, the wind in the cracks,
the old books, the phonograph in the parlor,
her vision of them all, glorious and loving.
In its name she kept her mother alive
on chickenfood and vitamins.
She thought she was nourishing a saint.
Grandma, that old crafty intellectual pirate,
she knew what it was about. Simply one more way
of getting fall-down drunk on sentiment.

And in its name my father shot himself and his secretary.
Behaviorism and science
are not enough to save from the cannibal ego.

They wring their hands when none of the furious
dreams come true.
And not that anything fails to come about because of their
lack of zeal!
God! Effort is the lodestar of their lives.
Enlisted in an endless civil war against reality
of which each act is a prodigy of humorless sweat,
and wildly pursuing the bright stars of the Christmas sparklers,
laying hand on the hot metal—mistaking the agony for truth—
determined to think that what the senses know—is a dream—
and what is only dreamed—is the true flesh and bone—
they are eternally astounded when
the face of the torturer unmasks and is goodwill—
their own.

One day in Alabama when the Johnson grass by the railyard
was green on the slag-pile,
one day in Birmingham Alabama
in an old green Plymouth, I was a witness.
a deputy of the sheriff's, dressed as neatly as a clerk,
knocked about in the street two dead-drunk colored men
who scraped the fender of their car on mine.
And when I testified what happened at the trial,
and later they had sued him on his bond,
that man came down to my room with warm hurt eyes,
I swear he was a very gentle man, and said
"Now how you can do this to me I don't see,
to testify for two drunk niggers.
Don't you know I got a family?
I done it only as a favor to you,
I ask you now, what business was it of mine?
Me off duty taking my wife for a drive!—
I only got in it to help you, man—
ain't you got a religion?
Ain't you never heard of the Golden Rule?"

So once a day, with all these things in mind,
I take a handful of dirt, of skin,
and I say to myself "Here, right here, this is the place."

Some families are born without fingers,
some people are born without senses. Which is sad.

But I think there is a much more terrible thing,
—to be reared without one's own consent
in the cave of the mind like a faded fish
and to go as assuredly blind in the soul as a saint.

II

In this ugly foreign city where I've come to be
          more or less at home,
to which I was shot upward
like a flaming lava bomb
spat out of that toothless zealous crater-mouth,
out of that virulent volcanic pumice-scatter of hell-fire talk
and abused feeling, I go on being the projectile.
I go on roaring up, trying not to notice,
(little man that I am, in my fantasy I weigh three
          thousand pounds
and fleck off skins of blue fire as I boom in the middle
          of the state fair)
I seem to be flying forever higher and higher,
—will I never come to rest?

And when I wake up late at night and think where am I,
and what is about to happen and who will help me,
and I don't know, I think
if only there weren't so much to love about them.
Where did it start, this anathemata of the real?
One great aunt who lived at the time of the war
wrote forty years ago "the life of the slaves with kind
masters and mistresses is an epic that causes the history
of the South to stand out in the history of nations
as unique as a lovely poem. And it has made me glad
twice; to have known it in its romantic beauty and to know
it had to end to wipe out that blot upon a nation's honor."
And my grandfather, remembering the same times,
seeing them with another eye of witness—
"Several times on my way to school I saw the body of a
criminal lying in the street, having received his just
deserts for his crime. I remember a bad and desperate
negro, Alex Mason, who was in jail—a company of
regulators went up to regulate him and he fought so
furiously they had to kill him. I remember the whites

and blacks rioting in the streets—"
Where did it start?
I suppose it was all in that forbidden fun,
for amusement and money,
when they sold the first cargo on the Congo.
Whisky for the chief, gold and women for the crew.
A fortune for the Portsmouth Puritan
commanding the Brigantine.
All for fun—
And fun not being allowed for in the rules.

This is my South!
What do I do about it?
How do I get this belonging out of my belly?
Someone speaks of it,
there's a luckless minute when the anger goes away
and nothing is left but the Thanksgiving table,
the warm smells and the sounds of people,
the aunts, uncles, brothers, sisters,
fathers and mothers, all of them
eating and drinking, cracking the bones of life
in the name of Service and Our Father and Right.
All for fun, that isn't allowed for in the rules,
everything turning to moral service—like murder.
—to drink to forget we drink to forget we live.
My God, stop operating Doctor Schweitzer,
putting that steel plate front to back in our heads.
It makes us able to go on drinking death
and never connecting with the taste of it.

Zeppelin

Someone has built a dirigible in my parlor.
What on earth has happened to the boarders?
I go in there sometimes
and tear the fabric off the framework, I shout
"who's responsible for this?"
but nobody answers.

There's nothing underneath
but a wilderness of girders
and a gas bag without any gas.
The dog has taken to living in one of my shoes.
Poor thing! His blanket was by the fireplace,
now filled up with the underfin.
When the propellers turn they open the doors,
they scatter papers down the hall to the garden,
sometimes they blow the paper I'm reading into my face.
My first editions are soggy with crankcase oil,
and the batik shawl I brought from ancient Mesopotamia
is soaked in grease.
Up there the pointed cone upon the nose
protrudes through my Matisse.
The pilot (at least I suppose he's the pilot)
is balled up on my bed, and when I shake him
he lifts one flap of his aviator's tarboosh to shout
"I didn't do it" and something that sounds like
"metal fatigue." He burrows into my pillow
deeper with his head. I saw a man in a mechanic's uniform
climb up inside this morning. I said
"Look here now, this is my living room!"
He only banged with his wrench,
shook his fist at my fractured plaster and shouted
"what's important is that in the end it fly."
I have to admire his singleness of mind.
Why it isn't even a new model. "Gott straff England"
is written across the gondola with lipstick in gothic lettering.
One of these mornings I've got to get out and see my lawyer.
Maybe he will suggest somebody to sue.
In the meantime for my conscience' sake
I need someone authoritative to tell me
what are the principles involved,
I mean so I will know if I should
feel resentful or honored.

James Baker Hall

The Poet Finds an Ephemeral Home in a Truck Stop
on the New Jersey Turnpike, ca. 1970

FOR BOB HOLMAN

Just look out there in the lot, dozens
of trailer trucks, each of them
covered with road dirt: monumental
cartes blanches is what they are!
I see myself out there zapped up
like a bill-board painter writing poems
on the dirty sides of those trailers
with my finger. I write, Title:
Introduction to Transcentental Numbers:
Poem: The greatness of living in Dwarf, Ky.
is all the others who aren't! Love, Jimmy.

Just think of all the people who'll read that!
Abstract expressionism in the Chase Manhattan,
and now poetry, poetry! on M & M trucks—
America by God will make it yet!

Picture the Babcocks, all seven of them
in their relatively new station wagon
passing my introductory poem on the way
to Grandma's house in Wilkes-Barre, Pa.,
picture that will you!
                         And picture
eighteen year old Wayne Willis and his girl
sitting close in his souped up GTO
with a license plate that reads LUV ONE
in Topeka, Kansas, he and his girl
pull up beside my big trucking poem
at a stoplight in Topeka, Kansas . . .

dozens and dozens of poems, each
with a specific destination unknown
to me, au courant! I'm so excited!
I love "Sailing to Byzantium," I really do,
but times have a-changed! Take art
out from behind the glass! No more
corrasable bond, no more agents
and editors and all that New York shit!

Straight to Topeka, Kansas, to Wayne Willis,
and old Wayne and his girl, pulling
up beside my big poem, they'll see
how the letters are all equally clear,
and he'll say to his girl, Gee whiz,
that poet who found the ephemeral home
in the truck stop on the Jersey Turnpike
licks his motherhunching finger
after every letter, he's eating
America's road dirt for us! And
his girl will say, For us and
for his motherhunching art too!
Your preoccupation with pure motives,
Wayne, is a drag.
                    And when I hear that
I'll know that I've arrived!
A mixed-media extravaganza, not
just words but calligraphy, the letters
themselves calligraphic analogues
to the poem's experience; and theater too,
a moving stage cannily subverting the old
tight-ass audience/art object relationship—

And so I up quick with another poem, it says,
Boston Bruins, #1, But You Know That!

And it's so clear now that I know
what I'm doing, that I'm where it's at—
consecrating our daily experience
with my art—that my next says simply,

Wayne Willis in souped up GTO and
girl sitting close in Topeka, Kansas,
I love you!

            And when they see that,
they say, Wow, did you see *that*?

William Harmon

The Dawn Horse

Again the time and blood consuming sun crosses its corner
with a web of new born light
and there the last stars literally starve

Grey among a hundred or so other greys
the dawn horse stirs

wakes to the waking manifold of new circumstance
and—totally inhuman and remote
among deep empty drums of sound unreeling hungrily
    as though long drowned or long ago
    among unsteady equinoctial darknesses—
stands

On the welcoming west slope of the world's first mountain
half dark in the tilted dominion of imperial light and common grasses
he is standing up
    as dew will stand on the difficult pitched deck of grass
    in the looking light

an ordinary model of simplicity
spotted
    as when water spots a smooth leaf
    with many magnifying glasses
    that evaporate in place
    or else slip in the inflammatory turn and sloping
cold
solid enough for anybody

Not one that waits at a fence for forked hay
or feedbag of fodder hung on a headstall in a stable
it is only he
the ghostly dawn horse
not maiden white but stone colored

Not a martingale gnawing nightmare
or rainbow shouldered unicorn at ambiguous attention

but a shaking shadow
    like the remote beating of the timed beast heart
begotten and blessed by something
blooded and blood loving

Lowering his head for a moment
he starts to step

To Redound

Responsively
Our whole house shakes to the thunder's psalm,

Windows react
To the wind's offices, and I am turned all the way around

By the bold sound
That represents, in one sense, almost nothing at all,

In another sense,
The presence of one of the old popular gods,

Avuncular,
Gullible, petty, sports-minded, omnipotent, girl-crazy,

But nothing now
But noise to us, with some nominal vestiges of awe.

One could tell it
To roar on. Lord Byron told the deep blue sea to roll,

Longfellow told
The flower of the lily to bloom on. Romanticism

Consists in things
Of that sort. Redundant. So, what the hell. Throw

Your hammer, Thor!
Thunder, thunder. Provoke apostrophes. Be yourself. That's it.

WILLIAM HARMON

Literacy: An Abandoned Ode

FOR MAX STEELE

Poems have become so boring to me
I have quit worrying with them.
I read, needless to say, a great deal
Anyhow (you all), but no poems.

I will talk to them, for a change,
And tell them that I can see quite through them,
Sleeves made of amplified trampolines
Like glass showcases full of glass geese,
Metaphors like successful anacondas
Processing some more or less innocent
Example of local fauna—
Enough!

The universe is one long *National Geographic.*
Or else, the universe is one long clothesline
Running from the front porch of a grocery store
To a coil of *Reader's Digests* ready at the left hand
of God the Father Almighty.

The many-colored clothes hang in no wind.
Enough.

Prose? Prose I can still manage to handle
Well enough—until, that is,
The first name surfaces.
When *Wilbur Bigelow opens the door* though
I close the book.

The natural state of books
Is shut, after all,
As of people, asleep. . . .

Mothsong

Some dust,

such as it is,
is transferred from a mother's album
to a son's turning finger,

then from the finger
to the front of a dark coat,
once a father's,

and then from there, some months later,
to the substance that is found
on a newborn moth's wing,

witnessed intermittently from below
colliding fitfully with the frosted globe
of a fixture
in the middle of a kitchen ceiling,

an irregular but redundant disturbance,
turning, stubborn,
a tolling of sorts, or
a knocking,

like something asymmetrical happening,

the song of an old fork
going downstairs.

And so from that moth now
back to this paper,
not so far after all
from the heavy black pages
of a mother's album under a table lamp,

bland public paper
here in the hand,
to be balled up,
a fist, a mind,
a clenched white apple
hanging in a darkening orchard.

Donald Justice

Beyond the Hunting Woods

I speak of that great house
Beyond the hunting woods,
Turreted and towered
In nineteenth-century style,
Where fireflies by the hundreds
Leap in the long grass,
Odor of jessamine
And roses, canker-bit,
Recalling famous times
When dame and maiden sipped
Sassafras or wild
Elderberry wine,
While far in the hunting woods
Men after their red hounds
Pursued the mythic beast.

I ask it of a stranger,
In all that great house finding
Not any living thing,
Or of the wind and the weather,
What charm was in that wine
That they should vanish so,
Ladies in their stiff
Bone and clean of limb,
And over the hunting woods
What mist had maddened them
That gentlemen should lose
Not only the beast in view
But Belle and Ginger too,
Nor home from the hunting woods
Ever, ever come?

In Bertram's Garden

Jane looks down at her organdy skirt
As if *it* somehow were the thing disgraced,
For being there, on the floor, in the dirt,
And she catches it up about her waist,
Smooths it out along one hip,
And pulls it over the crumpled slip.

On the porch, green-shuttered, cool,
Asleep is Bertram, that bronze boy,
Who, having wound her around like a spool,
Sends her spinning like a toy
Out to the garden, all alone,
To sit and weep on a bench of stone.

Soon the purple dark will bruise
Lily and bleeding-heart and rose,
And the little Cupid lose
Eyes and ears and chin and nose,
And Jane lie down with others soon
Naked to the naked moon.

The Assassination

It begins again, the nocturnal pulse.
It courses through the cables laid for it.
It mounts to the chandeliers and beats there, hotly.
We are too close. Too late, we would move back.
We are involved with the surge.

Now it bursts. Now it has been announced.
Now it is being soaked up by newspapers.
Now it is running through the streets.
The crowd has it. The woman selling carnations
And the man in the straw hat stand with it in their shoes.

Here is the red marquee it is sheltered under,
Here is the ballroom, here

The sadly various orchestra led
By a single gesture. My arms open.
It enters. Look, we are dancing.

June 5, 1968

David Kirby

The Schloss

The chutes are tiny smoke puffs against the dark Bavarian sky the credits
are still rolling but you know that it's only minutes until the commandoes
garrote the teenaged sentry who is dreaming of his mother force the slim
ascetic looking colonel to release the Allied scientist and for good measure
toss grenades into the room where the drunken officers are flirting with
the whores from town stray shots hit the gas main the whole thing goes up
in flames blink that's the partisans' signal and soon the commandoes are
on their way to the secret airfield now they're scrambling into the plane
but the leader hears engines it's the soldiers who got away a flare lights
the sky and suddenly everybody's shooting the partisan captain's beret
falls off and hey it's a woman the commando leader grabs her hand but
the plane begins to taxi and the partisan captain shouts there's no time
and the leader says I'll be back and they're in the air the leader helpless
as the partisans and the Germans have it out on the ground and while the
partisans appear to be winning he isn't sure but he thinks he sees her fall
and now for a few questions like who shot Travis was Carruther's death
really an accident and why were the sentry posts changed at the last minute
someone isn't on the level here and the leader knows who it is so he lists
the survivors one by one until he reaches Cummings who grabs a gun
and says he'll shoot the scientist right in the ear and blow those key formulae
right to hell unless the plane heads for Berlin at once so the plane banks
sharply and whoops there goes Cummings out the door that they didn't close
on takeoff while the commandoes all jump on the scientist who gets bruised
a little but at least he doesn't fall out as the plane makes a slow wide turn
toward England and you breathe for what seems like the first time in hours
even though you've seen this movie dozens of times before each time cursing
the deaths of Travis and Carruthers applauding the daring rescue wondering
whether the partisan captain survived and if the commando leader came
back when the war was over you even ask yourself who won for Christ's
sake and that's when you realize how sleepy you've become and how much
you need to rest before reveille a last minute briefing in which you finally
tell the others about the schloss some coffee and a biscuit a quick check of
the chutes and supplies and then the long silent flight into the winter sky

The Briefing

The tyrants are meeting, the bastards,
and each has a funny quirk:
a tic, a missing limb, an accent,
an odd affectation of dress,
a hostile-looking pet of some kind.
"Chentlemen," says the head tyrant,
a bald guy with a monocle and
dueling scars, "ve must begin":
wall panels open, a light beam
shoots out of a hidden projection booth,
and suddenly the tyrants are looking
at a picture of you. They twist in their seats
and murmur to one another;
the ones who have pets begin to stroke them
nervously. Your face has shaken them:
the eyes are deadly, the hair full of menace,
and for a single terrified moment,
the villains share this thought:
that "none of us is safe while she lives."

Etheridge Knight

The Idea of Ancestry

1

Taped to the wall of my cell are 47 pictures: 47 black
faces: my father, mother, grandmothers (1 dead), grand
fathers (both dead), brothers, sisters, uncles, aunts,
cousins (1st & 2nd), nieces, and nephews. They stare
across the space at me sprawling on my bunk. I know
their dark eyes, they know mine. I know their style,
they know mine. I am all of them, they are all of me;
they are farmers, I am a thief, I am me, they are thee.

I have at one time or another been in love with my mother,
1 grandmother, 2 sisters, 2 aunts (1 went to the asylum),
and 5 cousins. I am now in love with a 7 yr old niece
(she sends me letters written in large block print, and
her picture is the only one that smiles at me).

I have the same name as 1 grandfather, 3 cousins, 3 nephews,
and 1 uncle. The uncle disappeared when he was 15, just took
off and caught a freight (they say). He's discussed each year
when the family has a reunion, he causes uneasiness in
the clan, he is an empty space. My father's mother, who is 93
and who keeps the Family Bible with everybody's birth dates
(and death dates) in it, always mentions him. There is no
place in her Bible for "whereabouts unknown."

2

Each Fall the graves of my grandfathers call me, the brown
hills and red gullies of Mississippi send out their electric
messages, galvanizing my genes. Last yr/like a salmon quitting
the cold ocean—leaping and bucking up his birthstream/I
hitchhiked my way from L.A. with 16 caps in my pocket and a
monkey on my back and I almost kicked it with the kinfolks.
I walked barefooted in my grandmother's backyard/I smelled the old
land and the woods/I sipped cornwhiskey from fruit jars with the men/
I flirted with the women/I had a ball till the caps ran out
and my habit came down. That night I looked at my grandmother
and split/my guts were screaming for junk/but I was almost
contented/I had almost caught up with me.
(The next day in Memphis I cracked a croaker's crib for a fix.)

This yr there is a gray stone wall damming my stream, and when
the falling leaves stir my genes, I pace my cell or flop on my bunk
and stare at 47 black faces across the space. I am all of them,
they are all of me, I am me, they are thee, and I have no sons
to float in the space between

Duane Locke

A Bullfrog in a Pond Not Far from an Abandoned Farm

I watched a bullfrog and entered his dark water
I kept the brownness
found among the green of the stone's lichen
My fingers and the fern that grows from the stone
were the same
My ancestors' voices were still
in the grass of this pasture
and they brought a pack of dogs
to bite the silence
They offered me their gifts
a cow bell a horse whip the pig's snout ring
I sent my eyes into the frog's eyes
let his waters open my skin and enter
I heard the walking canes of the blind
tap the floors of my blood vessels
Their shoes were heavy and warm
I saw the sun come up from a sand grain
and streak the water above me
with gold cypresses

Ybor City

The antique lights
still there,
but
the checker boards
have buried
their scarves and berets.
The bread
by the coffee cup
grown stale.
It has become stone
and cannot break
into crumbs.
The sparrows peck

and break their bills.
The lost sweater
on the sidewalk
mumbled, "Change.
Everything changes."
We pick up
our bicycles
and from the closed shop
depart.

Jeff Daniel Marion

My Grandmother Sifting

years of the world's distance
glazed
behind panes of darkness

now
near the cupboard
she goes by the feel
of flour sifting

touch by touch
the world enters here
descending in whiteness
across her hands

a winter sky shakes itself loose:
drift of last summer's
dust in a cold season

where morning stokes its light
across her sills
in patchwork

alone daily
she
breaks this bread

Jim Wayne Miller

The Bee Woman

She carried the eggs in her straw hat and never
reached into a nest with her bare hand.
A woman who could conjure warts, who knew
charms for drawing fire, spells to make
butter come, and mysteries of bees
and hummingbirds, besides, knew to roll
eggs from a guinea's nest with a gooseneck hoe.

There is a mountain cove and light is leaving.
Speckled guineas fly to roost in trees,
their potterick and screech drifts far away,
becomes the faintest peeping in my dream
of stifling afternoons when we would stand,
the old woman and I, by fencerows and cowtrails
listening for half-wild guineas screeching
as they came off nests they'd stolen away
in thickets, briers, scrub pines, and chinquapins.

And no matter where I wake—horn's beep,
ship's bells, clatter of garbage cans,
strange tongues spoken on the street below,
in a rising falling bunk out at sea—
everywhere I stand on native ground.
The bee woman may pass through my dream:
running under a cloud of swarming bees,
she beats an empty pie pan with a spoon
till the swarm settles, black on a drooping pine bough
and guineas regroup pottericking—all
moving toward waking's waterfall.

Squirrel Stand

Now burley's curing in the high-tiered barn
and yellow leaves ride out on slow black water.
Cold wind moving in the rows of corn
rattles the blades like an old man pulling fodder.
Down from the mountain pastures overnight,

cattle stand by the yellow salt block bawling.
Now it's September in the world; fine rain is falling.

—When gray squirrels had grown fat on hickory nuts,
my gun in the crook of my arm, once I went stepping
through yellow leaves and fine rain falling.
Resting on a ridge above our tents,
I heard what raincrows off in the mist were calling:
my days were growing full, sliding, dropping
like waterbeads along the barbed-wire fence.

Jim Worley Fries Trout on South Squalla

I

I was bear huntin
about four five miles from here,
it was in November.
Commenced to sleet
tickin in the leaves
and I follered a branch down
come on a cabin.
Didn't know anybody was livin back in there.
Nobody to home but a woman
and her boy—about eight year old.
That woman's tits hung down
like sticks of baloney
and that boy could nuss her
standing flat-footed on the floor,
and did, by God, an me a-standing there.
Never saw nothin like it.

Never did know where her old man was,
never ast. Hell, I was bear huntin.
Besides that boy was eight or nine year old,
like I said. Pass me that salt.
Do you like right much salt?

II

Bunch of hippies come in the county back
about two year ago. Cocksuckers.
They was a old hippie was the ringleader,
grayheaded little bastard, hair down to his shoulder,
and I reckon he had money. From New York
or off yonder somewhers. Bought some of that
land the lumber company sold at auction.
Next thing you knowed, goddam hippies
was comin in from all over,
hitch-hikin, packs on their backs,
I saw a bunch get out of a VW bus
was like a holler log packed full of coons,
big-bottom pants and flowerdy shirts,
bands around their hair like Injins—
wearin necklaces. They was all livin up there
on that old hippie's land, in tents, lean-tos,
under rocks. Started buildin a house, more like
a long shed with ten or fifteen rooms.
Feller I know hauled lumber up there to em.

Turned out they wasn't just hippies
by god they's nudistes to boot.
After they built that bunkhouse
they planted little garden patches.
You could come in from that back side
and go along the ridge and see em workin
them garden patches nekkid as jaybirds
or layin in the sun on matresses, like lizards,
hair plumb down to the crack of their ass
and you couldn't tell the boys from the girls
till they turned over. And then you had to look
through the scope of a deer rifle.

Well, sir, one night last spring a bunch went up there
and burnt em out. They're still some old half-burnt-up
mattresses layin around up there they tried to pull out
but the bunkhouse it burnt down.
Said hippies come pourin out that shed
like bees smoked out of a beetree.

That old hippie I reckon he still does own the place
but none's been up there since.

That old hippie he posted his land, by god,
didn't want nobody huntin nor fishin on the place.
I believe that's what turned people agin him.
Goddam, folks won't put up with that in this county.

You know what'd really be good?
Some little spring onions to cut up in that grease.

Vassar Miller

The Ghostly Beast

My broken bones cry out for love
To bind me tighter than a glove,
Whereas I scarcely feel your hand
Bestowing what my bones demand.

I have no origin nor end
Within your heart's deep night unpenned;
You pick me up to set me down
Where I in seas of freedom drown.

Your weight withdrawn weighs burdensome
Upon my flesh till I become
The interval between two breaths,
A life lived out in little deaths.

Your airy fingers rub me raw
More than wolf's fang or tiger's claw;
The shadows of your passing rip
Skin from my body like a whip.

Distilling dew into a wine,
You make me grosser than a swine;
You feast me on platonic fare
Until I turn into a bear.

Though my protest may be no crisper
In your dominions than a whisper,
In rhymes like catapulted stones
My love cries out for broken bones.

On Approaching My Birthday

My mother bore me in the heat of summer
when the grass blanched under sun's hammer stroke
and the birds sang off key, panting between notes,
and the pear trees once all winged with whiteness
sagged, breaking with fruit, and only the zinnias,
like harlots, bloomed out vulgar and audacious,

and when the cicadas played all day long
their hidden harpsichords accompanying
her grief, my mother bore me, as I say,
then died shortly thereafter, no doubt
of her disgust and left me her disease
when I grew up to wither into truth.

A Lesson in Detachment

She's learned to hold her gladness lightly,
Remembering when she was a child
Her fingers clenched a bird too tightly,
And its plumage, turned withered leaf,
No longer fluttered wild.

Sharper than bill or claw, her grief
Needled her palm that ached to bleed,
And could not, to assuage the grief
Pulsations of the tiny scrap
Crumpled against her need.

To prison love: a tiny snap
Of iron to be forged a band,
A toy to prove one day a trap
Destined to close without a qualm
Upon itself, her hand.

She bids her clutching five grow calm
Lest in their grip a wing might buckle
Beyond repair, and for her balm
She'll cup no joy now in her palm,
But perch it on her knuckle.

Spinster's Lullaby
FOR JEFF

Clinging to my breast, no stronger
Than a small snail snugly curled,
Safe a moment from the world,
Lullaby a little longer.

Wondering how one tiny human
Resting so, on toothpick knees
In my scraggly lap, gets ease,
I rejoice, no less a woman

With my nipples pinched and dumb
To your need whose one word's sucking.
Never mind, though. To my rocking
Nap a minute, find your thumb

While I gnaw a dream and nod
To the gracious sway that settles
Both our hearts, imperiled petals
Trembling on the pulse of God.

William Mills

Pity

She asked me twice
Didn't I kill the
Catfish
Before I took the pliers
And stripped his hide.
I said no,
You'd have to break his neck.
I, now uneasy,
Blood bright on my fingers
Saw her wince,
The whiskered fish
Twisting.
Looks like torture that way,
She said,
And I said look
If you ask that question
It leads to another.
This is the way it's done.

Marion Montgomery

Aunt Emma, Uncle Al: A Short History of the South

My Uncle Al on Saturday night lay warmly in the ditch
and Sunday morning saw the Lordly Tisking church-
ward
While Aunt Emma kept the sentimental lamp bright into
breakfast;

And Sunday morning Uncle Al tied grannyknots and
squareknots and flipped nickels up his sleeve. He told
about that marvelous old unicorn, the hoop snake of
the ivory horn and apple tree
While Aunt Emma piled plates, rejoicing Uncle Al out
under arbor shooting marbles with his boys;

And Uncle Al called quail up in the orchard in the after-
noon and sang the moon up with his brood around him
on the steps
While Aunt Emma bathed the barefoot sleepy feet;

Until a solemn Sunday when the Lordly Tisking raised
my Uncle Al up from the ditch. The two to twelve to
teens scrubbed necks for Sunday School while Aunt
sweating Emma fried chicken for my Lordly Tisking
Uncle Al.

Lost marbles, squareknots only, and the aphids sucked the
scuppernongs.

And when Aunt Emma died with cancer of the womb the
three to teens began to scatter like flushed quail

And all my Uncle Al's sharp evening calling never
brought them back to roost again.

Robert Morgan

Topsoil

Sun's heat collects in leaf crystals
crumbling.
Earth grinds the grain
to dark flour, drifts black flannel
over rock and clay.
Life invests
and draws on.
A lake rises over the world,
heaps of the rotting ocean.
Suns' heat adding
weight
piles on its light
century after century tarnishing
earth's metal.
Traffic of roots
hurrying. Places the raw meat
shows through torn to the quick.
Red clay mirrors.
Black fruit
growing around the earth, deepening
in the autumn
sun drifting down.

Hogpen

In the pine woods, at the log
enclosure with a roof
over one corner,
you can get up close
to the grunting breather.
And he knows you're there, always
watching through a chink.
Suddenly whirls
his great weight
squealing to the other
side, for all his size quick

as a cat; stands
in mud plush.
Living out
our exile we come
with offerings
of scraps, bran.
Slopped over and gomming
his snout he's after
it so fast, snorkeling
under, coughing.
Licks the trough bare to
meal stuck in cracks,
clabber whitening
hoofpools.
Sun brews the
tincture, flies steaming.
A scree of cobs bleaches downhill
where canfuls of worms can
be dug every foot.
It's a good place to play on
a hot day, in the pines,
spice of needles,
resin swelling.
Play close to the slow
talker
panting behind the logs.
He listens, taking
an interest.
Stirs in the inner
chambers, blessing the hours.

Steep

Driven out from the centers of population,
displaced from villages and crossroads and too poor
to acquire the alluvial bottomlands,
the carbon-dark fields along the creek,

forced back on the rocky slopes above branches,
to the flanks near the headwaters,
pushed to the final mountain wall, I brace
my faculties against falling out of labor

and prop up or stake down every stalk, dig
terraces and drive fences to save what little
topsoil there is from the gullywashers
hitting almost every afternoon up here in summer.

Cow trails babel the steepest knobs, make
by spiral and switchback the sheer peaks
and outcroppings accessible. I plant only root
vegetables, turnips, potatoes, and prehensile creepers.

Too far to carry whole or raw things
into town, I take the trouble only with something
boiled down, distilled, and clear new
ground every three or four years.

I live high on the hogback near
dividing water, I disaffiliate and secede.
I grow ginseng in hollows unlit as the dark
side of the moon, and confederate with moisture and

insular height to bring summit orchards
to bear. I husband the scartissue of erosion.

Dark Corner

Was said around home nobody
lived in Dark Corner, just
near it. For us it was across
the ridge in South Carolina.
After dark with the wind right
you could tell somebody was making.
Strong as the fermenting shade
under an appletree
fumes came chimneying
through the gap in Painter

Mountain. Whole cornfields asweat
through an eye. What focus!
Not to mention sunlight gathered on the hillsides
by the flush of cornleaves, and ground water
freighting minerals taken by sucker
roots, long weeks of play
with hoe and cultivator before
the laying by; stalks stretching
exhilarate in the July night
till sun fills the cobs' teeth
with oil. No mention
of top cutting,
fodder pulling. Talk
of digestion in mash vats at the head
of the holler, sugar agitations,
transubstantiations, work
of bacterial excitements till
hot sweetness arrives. Comes the runoff
calling from the corruptions and burning
a ghost returned by the reflector
to a cool point. Manifests
heavy drops, pore
runny with lunar ink.

Back up under the summit line
where smoke is hid by haze
and updrafts lift
the mash smell a few
hundred yards out of state,
the lookout waits on the laurel ledge,
gun in lap to fire warning.
A rattler suns near, his crevice
high over the settlement.
Down there houses propped, a toilet
wades the creek on stilts. Man
here'll go down
on his daughter, god
damn her soul.

Uncle got sent up for moonshine,
did time in the Atlanta pen.
Long as water runs and corn grows green

and fire boils water I'll be making,
Judge, reckon on it, he said.
But something there broke him.
Rumor blamed the whippings. He
came back old, a new man.

Paul Baker Newman

Skimmers

Where you see the undersides of their wings
the flock is white and flickering in the sunlight
above the sandbar and the blue water of the sound
and you can hear them crying and protesting
in the cool sea wind that blows across the channel,
and where the rest of them are turning toward you
they are all black and flickering in the sunlight
and they go swinging in a long Cartesian figure
like a twisted plane that lets you see its outlines
by its colors, the one half white and tilting away,
and the other half black and tilting toward you,
as they swing into the air and call you all the names
they can think of in the time it takes to rise
and get away, loping on their long black wings
so leisurely toward the sound behind the islands.

Washington on the Constitutional Journey: 1791

Up from the mud among the fiddlers
they follow the corduroy road.
The calamus leaves are tipping

in the wind from the sea, and the marsh
grass makes a slow rustling
in the long gusts that riffle up

the current. They are following
a straight road across the rice-fields
with the horse snorting at the logs

half-buried in mud, and the black-
birds singing in the cat-tails
and the dragonflies as swift as fish

that see you and are gone with one swish
of their tails. He must remember to praise
those who were for the Constitution.

126

It takes a particular man to raise
rice in all this mud and choose right.
The sun and the clouds are fighting for the river,

as they approach the South Santee,
turning brown and silver as the light
hits it direct or filters through a cloud.

Sam Ragan

That Summer

That summer when the creeks all dried up
Except for a few deep holes
Under the caved-out roots of oaks
Now leaning toward the water's edge,
The catfish clung to the mud,
But now and then a perch was caught
In the oatsack seine.
Even the Tar was a trickle,
And I could walk all the way across
On the rocks. The place
Where we had swung from limb to water,
Splashing below surface and rising sputtering,
Was now just mud
From which a turtle crawled.
     They sat on the porches
     And talked of the weather
     And Herbert Hoover,
     Cursing both and every son of a bitch
     Who had voted for him.
     Even if the Baptists saved any souls
     Worth the saving
     Where in the hell would they find
     Enough water to baptize them?
A wild turkey flew out of the woods.
It was out of season, but it fed
The family for two days.
It tasted better than the turtle
That looked like mud and tasted like mud.

Paul Ramsey

The Advent Images

Parched with age, in the quiet mist,
Women each year took images,
Mary and Jesus, house to house.
They walked through an English landscape
Past thinned streams, winter like shadow
That on brambles moves and wavers,
Earth withering, peaceful, and bare.
Advent is a spare season, fit
For penance, yet shall Christmas come
When a great log burns on the hearth
And the Christ awakes in the arms
Of her who bore us God, and we
May think of women who carry,
Far and glad, an awkward display.
Calmly through shadow they hasten
And call on us to behold God.

A Snowman in March

He is a sort of god.
Where slowly, dense, and cool
The deep lawn of snow thaws,
This craggy snowman, odd
As a trick of eye, stands,
Capricious as applause,
Idle martyr and fool,
With head half gone, no hands.
The seeds await his nod.

Julia Randall

To William Wordsworth from Virginia

I think, old bone, the world's not with us much.
I think it is too difficult to see,
But easy to discuss. Behold the bush.
His seasons out-maneuver Proteus.
This year, because of the drought, the barberry
Is all goldflakes in August, but I'll still say
To the First Grade next month, "*Now* it is Fall.
You see the leaves go bright, and then go small.
You see October's greatcoat. It is gold.
It will lie on the earth to keep the seed's foot warm.
Then, Andrew Obenchain, what happens in June?"
And Andrew, being mountain-bred, will know
Catawba runs too deep for the bus to get
Across the ford—at least it did last May,
And school was out, and the laundry wouldn't dry,
And when the creek went down, the bluebells lay
In Hancock's pasture-border, thick as hay.

What do they tell the First Grade in Peru,
I wonder? All the story: God is good,
He counts the children, and the sparrow's wing.
God loved William Wordsworth in the spring.
William Wordsworth had enough to eat.
Wye was his broth, Helvellyn was his meat,
And English was his cookstove. And where did words
Come from, Carlyle Rucker? Words that slide
The world together. Words that split the tide
Apart for Moses (not for Mahon's bus),
Words that say, the bushes burn for us—
Lilac, forsythia, orange, Sharon rose—
For us the seasons wheel, the lovers wait,
All things become the flesh of our delight,
The evidence of our wishes.

                         Witch, so might
I stand beside the barberry and dream
Wisdom to babes, and health to beggar men,
And help to David hunting in the hills
The Appalachian fox. By words, I might.
But, sir, I am tired of living in a lake

Among the watery weeds and weedy blue
Shadows of flowers that Hancock never grew.
I am tired of my pet wishes, of running away
Like all the nymphs, from the droughty eye of day.
Run, Daphne. Run, Europa, Io, run!
There is not a god left underneath the sun
To balk, to ride, to suffer, to obey.
Here is the unseasonable barberry.
Here is the black face of a child in need.
Here is the bloody figure of a man.
Run, Great Excursioner. Run if you can.

Rockland

Masters, be kind to the old house that must fall,
Burn, or be bulldozed. The apples have grown small
And the ivy great here. The walk must be moved once more
Beyond the holly. Do not use the side door,
The lilies have broken the step. If you fix it,
They will break it again; they live under the stone.
There is blown glass
In three windows; hold them up with a stick.
The smoke is always thick
With the first fire. The Landseer in the attic
Was tacked there when I came. There is a snake
With a red tongue in the terrace; he has never been known
To hurt. The worst leak
Is in the bedroom ceiling. So. It was a good house
For hands to patch, a boon to August eyes. And when
The moon lay on the locusts, and the stream
Croaked in the bottom, muted by high grass,
Small rustlings in the woodlot, birdcries, was
A minister like music. Should I say
This—with the apple tree—was Sirmio,
This—with the two-year parsley—Twickenham,
Aldworth, or Abbotsford, I would only mean
We lease one house in love's divided name.

A Ballad of Eve

The blessed worm of Eden sang
At my immortal ear:
The rose will riot on the vine
Year after year;

Night after night in love unbought
The man beside you lie,
And children run on painless feet
Around you day by day;

One god, of all the gods that be,
His table will suffice,
And hand and heart and tongue will know
no enemy but peace.

I walked alone into the dark,
Looking for my deed.
I struck my hand upon a rock
And could not make it bleed.

I lay across the lion's path
Who skirted softly on.
That whole wood was passionless
Up to the edge of dawn.

And there upon the bough it lay.
That made my first heart break.
With human hands I plucked the sky,
With human hunger ate.

And then such plenty was to do,
Danger and pride and pain,
It took me years to fashion true
God's dreaming song again,

The voice that doubled in my ear
Then, in my first of days,
And seasoned love with pity so
I had no tongue for praise,

That now sing back, daylong, the dark,
And nightlong sing the day
I walked the years from paradise
Where god beside me lay.

Gibbons Ruark

Sleeping Out with My Father

Sweet smell of earth and easy rain on
Canvas, small breath fogging up the lantern
Glass, and sleep sifting my bones, drifting me
Far from hide-and-seek in tangled hedges,
The chicken dinner with its hills of rice
And gravy and its endless prayers for peace,
Old ladies high above me creaking in the choir loft,
And then the dream of bombs breaks up my sleep,
The long planes screaming down the midnight
Till the whistles peel my skin back, the bombs
Shake up the night in a sea of lightning
And stench and spitting shrapnel and children
Broken in the grass, and I am running
Running with my father through the hedges
Down the flaming streets to fields of darkness,
To sleep in sweat and wake to news of war.

A Blind Wish for Randall Jarrell

Sometimes all the roads seem dark.

But in that darkness trees and animals
Take slow shape under an enormous will.

The field between the lost world and the world
You gently foundered in is woods again,

The bearded man and boy in tennis shoes
Now grow together in a single tree,

Or run with the blood of a single fox,
Leaping and falling in the deepening forest.

Impromptu Immersion in Tom's Run

Once somebody walked this Piney Mountain
Valley by the name of Tom. He must have known
This twisting run-off by its own right name,
Since afterward somebody named it for him.
I am up here following its silver
Whiplash for the first time. Hammer is good
Company, slow and garrulous as ever,
Stopping to fish in every pool of rain.
He fishes and I water down the drinks.
We slept last night inside the sound of water.
At dusk, the last light flashed from a wing-tip.
Now first sunlight stalks the creek-bed, warming
Us to hunger as we ramble downstream
Hunting for a trout pool. Nothing comes up,
Though Hammer says a trout could lie so still
In those cold shallows we would never see him.
Maybe so could I, I say, and strip down
Suddenly to nothing and am in it
Up to my knees, then flat-out on the stones,
Cunning and still as any mountain trout.
Climbing out I don't know what to call myself,
I feel so good in the growing sunlight.
I christen you nymph in the wood, says Hammer,
Who can't abide this craving after names.
If I caught a trout, he says, I'd call it trout.
Love, if I were with you by the ocean,
I'd lie down next to you and call it ocean.
Up here away from you, I can't let up.
What is the name of the strange white flower
On the forest floor? What is your own name?
I call that pool I bathed in Laurel Hole
For the one laurel over it, call myself
One solitude calling another home.

Larry Rubin

At the Birth of a Poet: Amherst, 1830

The guardians consult about the gifts to be
Bestowed. Angels can be generous if
The moon is right, the tides running brightly
To the sea. Wealth, rank, power—
The beauty of the bonds, the edge of gilt,
Industrial securities, textiles—
It is New England, after all. Yankee
Horse sense would have prevailed, no doubt,
But something in the texture of the house,
The garden, the quality of light, or perhaps
That infant's sherry eyes made them pause,
In jealousy that only angels feel.
"Textiles, yes!" cried one—"cloth so white
She'll wear it like a sister to the moon."
"Love is a gift for spirit eyes, let her
Have love," said another, a little sly.
"Not so fast," said the third, "I think
I'll starve that gift—let her be lean." "*Alone*,"
The chairman said, "My final word." "Words,"
The scribe wrote down. The list was done.

Saturday Afternoon

Rolling off the freeway, the football crowd
Got tangled with a funeral, diluting
Death till only the hearse could find the road.
The cars with lights got lost amidst the rush
To kickoff time, and whether some lucky
Mourners found themselves in bleacher seats
The Sunday papers never said. Absence
Is a minor thing, at funerals.

Yet touchdowns aren't really less eternal.
Tackles fall and ovals fly, yet something
In the autumn air isn't like a game.
The cheers roll on to victory, the poles

Come down, the hero slides off the shoulders
Of the crowd. Somewhere above the stadium
The shouts dissolve, and all the players dash
Through a little door, hidden in
A cellar wall. Beyond the line of scrimmage

An early dusk means headlights must go on,
All the same. Some may have missed the first
Handful of dirt, but there was sod enough
Upon that measured field; only buried
Captains know how many cubic yards.

The Runaway

The night he died, they sent me out for candles.
And that is when I heard the music sound
Where stars rode at anchor; everywhere
I heard that muffled band playing naval
Music, and saw him, cocky at sixteen,
Hoist his gear against his neck and stalk
Up the gangplank to see the world.
The stars danced, and he had girls, and I
Wasn't even born; but now above
The neon and the lights the sky is filled
With ships and my father struts with a sailor's gait
All night I hear the music through the candles,
And watch the ships move slowly past the stars.

God Opens His Mail

Dear Sir:
        Your poem interested us
Somewhat, but we do not consider it
Entirely successful. For one thing,
Your floral diction blooms in the right places,

But there are bugs which seem almost deliberately
Placed. Then, again, life breathes everywhere
In your work, yet you cancel it
Later in the lines with a disdain
No artist with a trace of self-respect
Would dare to show (not to mention compassion
For the child of his brain, but let
That pass). Do you have a friend
Who might perhaps be willing to read your work
Before you send it out? Just a suggestion,
But beginners must be guided. Another thing:
Your images, though pleasant taken singly,
Fail to fuse properly. We find a sly
Intent to suggest an overall design,
And yet the reader sees no real organic
Whole. Your metaphors stand isolated;
No poem can carry such disparities
As shooting stars and glory-holes, no matter
How securely yoked. Creation carries
Certain responsibilities, and we
Are unconvinced you have accepted these.
There are other problems, of course,
But our staff is limited, and time is short.
You have, we feel, much to learn, but your talent
Will help.
        Cordially,
          The Editors.

P.S. Since half the battle is knowing
Your market, perhaps you would care to subscribe.

Sonia Sanchez

a poem for my father

how sad it must be
to love so many women
to need so many black
perfumed bodies weeping
underneath you.
                    when i remember all those nights
i filled my mind with
long wars between short
sighted trojans & greeks
while you slapped some
wide hips about in
your pvt dungeon,
when i remember your
deformity   i want to
do something about your
makeshift manhood.
i guess
        that is why
on meeting your sixth
wife, i cross myself
with her confessionals.

George Scarbrough

Tenantry
(POLK COUNTY, TENNESSEE)

Always in transit
we were always temporarily
in exile,
each new place seeming
after a while
and for a while
our home.

Because no matter
how far we traveled
on the edge of strangeness
in a small county,
the earth ran before us
down red clay roads
blurred with summer dust,
banked with winter mud.

It was the measurable,
pleasurable earth
that was home.
Nobody who loved it
could ever be really alien.
Its tough clay, deep loam,
hill rocks, small flowers
were always the signs
of a homecoming.

We wound down through them
to them,
and the house we came to,
whispering with dead hollyhocks
or once in spring
sill-high in daisies,
was unimportant.
Wherever it stood,
it stood in earth,
and the earth welcomed us,
open, gateless,
one place as another.

And each place seemed
after a while
and for a while
our home:
because the county
was only a mansion
kind of dwelling
in which there were many
rooms.
We only moved from one
room to another,
getting acquainted
with the whole house.

And always the earth
was the new floor under us,
the blue pinewoods the walls
rising around us,
the windows the openings
in the blue trees
through which we glimpsed,
always farther on,
sometimes beyond the river,
the real wall of the mountain,
in whose shadow
for a little while
we assumed ourselves safe,
secure and comfortable
as happy animals
in an unvisited lair:

which is why perhaps
no house we ever lived in
stood behind a fence,
no door we ever opened
had a key.

It was beautiful like that.
For a little while.

Afternoon

I

Snow on my brother's grave
and a blue kite leveling
in the March wind.

Far off, the mountain
matches the blue kite
only as one spring another,
or the white church the snow.

Nearer, the child runs
unevenly over hummocks,
the air rattles with kite.

I brush the snow off our name.

II

How ox-blooded the air is
on the side of the hill
where he is buried,
as if the purple sedge
under duress of autumn
let burn into space
its color of cosmos.

He loved that flower.

III

We came here often,
autumn in our caps,
with gun, with holly.

Speckled things
live still, beyond
the thin Stonehenge
of our mountain,
And holly blooms.
But I hunt no more.
The land is posted
with his firstborn right.

IV

The shade of the green
catalpa is yellow,
the ghost of the green worm
is a spatter of gold.

In the sunshine there
is such an inweaving
of lithe gold shadows,
I see him climbing

Through green leaves,
through gold leaves, up,
upward, dream in
his gold eyes of

Gold fish for which
he harvests the lithe
spatters of sun from
the slimmest tops.

V

He offers me from
a plantation of dreams
a strong portion
of scarlet and yellow.

He tells me I
am not a man unless
I take his feast
without water,

And no tears. Only
boys cry, he says, from
his yellow landscape,
his scarlet sky.

Waking I hear
the autumn wind shake
the dry pepper pods
like paper.

James Seay

It All Comes Together Outside the Restroom in Hogansville

It was the hole for looking in
only I looked out
in daylight that broadened
as I brought my eye closer.
First there was a '55 Chevy
shaved and decked like old times
but waiting on high-jacker shocks.
Then a sign that said J. D. Hines Garage.
In J. D.'s door was an empty Plymouth
with the windows down and the radio on.
A black woman was singing in Detroit
in a voice that brushed against the face
like the scarf
turning up in the wrong suitcase
long ago after everything came to grief.
What was inside we can only imagine—
men I guess trying to figure what would make it
work again. Beyond them
beyond the cracked engine blocks and thrown pistons
beyond that failed restroom
etched with our acids beyond that American Oil Station
beyond the oil on the ground
the mobile homes all over Hogansville
beyond our longing
all Georgia was green.
I'd had two for the road
a cheap enough thrill
and I wanted to think
I could take only what aroused me.
The interstate to Atlanta was wide open.
I wanted a different life.
So did J. D. Hines. So did the voice on the radio.
So did the man or woman
who made the hole in the window.
The way it works is this:
we devote ourselves to an image
we can't live with and try to kill
anything that suggests it could be otherwise.

Grabbling in Yokna Bottom

The hungry come in a dry time
To muddy the water of this swamp river
And take in nets what fish or eel
Break surface to suck at this world's air.

But colder blood backs into the water's wood—
Gills the silt rather than rise to light—
And who would eat a cleaner meat
Must grabble in the hollows of underwater stumps and roots,

Must cram his arm and hand beneath the scum
And go by touch where eye cannot reach,
Must seize and bring to light
What scale or slime is touched—

Must in that instant—on touch—
Without question or reckoning
Grab up what wraps itself cold-blooded
Around flesh or flails the water to froth,

Or else feel the fish slip by,
Or learn that the loggerhead's jaw is thunder-deaf,
Or that the cottonmouth's fangs burn like heated needles
Even under water.

The well-fed do not wade this low river.

Edgar Simmons

At the Seed and Feed

Carrying his mandolin in the curve of the afternoon
Past the hot and shaded porch
Past flead dogs and the kings of bottletop checkers
Shooting their crowed eyes beyond their strawbrimmed hats
I followed my father into the dark of an old store.

Among men and tin and bottle goods
Among bonneted ladies with crochet hoops
White tambourines etched with blue flowers
We stood in Jesus-sweet gloom.

Now Father's wizard mandolin sings the store alive
The strings lightly throbbing,
Tinkling on and on, the frets marking his fleshy fingers
His notes like plums in the dark.

Soon a fox yelps down the evening
And cows loll home spearing from a covert of trees;
Now the piney church turns yellow for Wednesday prayers
And Father, slipping the pick under the mandolin strings, bows

Dwindling in the sun.

Dave Smith

Cumberland Station

Gray brick, ash, hand-bent railings, steps so big
it takes hours to mount them, polished oak
pews holding the slim hafts of sun, and one
splash of the *Pittsburgh Post-Gazette*. The man
who left Cumberland gone, come back, no job
anywhere. I come here alone, shaken
the way I came years ago to ride down
mountains in Big Daddy's cab. He was
the first set cold in the black meadow.

Six rows of track gleam, thinned, rippling
like water on walls where famous engines steam, half
submerged in frothing crowds with something
to celebrate and plenty to eat. One engineer takes
children for a free ride, a frolic
like an earthquake. Ash cakes their hair.
I am one of those who walked uphill
through flowers of soot to zing
scared to death into the world.

Now whole families afoot cruise South Cumberland
for something to do, no jobs, no money for bars,
the old stories cracked like wallets.

This time there's no fun in coming back. The second
death. My roundhouse uncle coughed his youth
into a gutter. His son, the third, slid on the ice,
losing his need to drink himself
stupidly dead. In this vaulted hall
I think of all the dirt poured down
from shovels and trains and empty pockets.
I stare into the huge malignant headlamps
circling the gray walls and catch a stuttered
glimpse of faces stunned like deer on a track,
children getting drunk, shiny as Depression apples.

Churning through the inner space of this godforsaken
wayside, I feel the ground try to upchuck and I dig
my fingers in my temples to bury a child
diced on a cowcatcher, a woman smelling
alkaline from washing out the soot.

Where I stood in that hopeless, hateful room
will not leave me. The scarf of smoke I saw
over a man's shoulder runs through me
like the sored Potomac River.

Grandfather, you ask why I don't visit you
now you have escaped the ticket-seller's cage
to fumble hooks and clean the Shakespeare reels.
What could we catch? I've been sitting in the pews
thinking about us a long time, long enough to see
a man can't live in jobless, friendless Cumberland
anymore. The soot owns even the fish.

I keep promising I'll come back, we'll get out,
you and me, like brothers, and I mean it.
A while ago a man with the look of a demented cousin
shuffled across this skittery floor and snatched up
the *Post-Gazette* and stuffed it in his coat
and nobody gave a damn because nobody cares
who comes or goes here or even who steals
what nobody wants: old news, photographs
of dead diesels behind chipped glass
swimming into Cumberland Station.

I'm the man who stole it and I wish you were here
to beat the hell out of me for it because
what you said a long time ago welts my face
and won't go away. I admit
it isn't mine even if it's nobody else's.
Anyway, that's all I catch this trip—bad
news. I can't catch my nephew's life, my uncle's,
Big Daddy's, yours, or the ash-haired kids'
who fell down to sleep here after the war.

Outside new families pick their way along tracks
you and I have walked home on many nights.
Every face on the walls goes on smiling,
and, Grandfather, I wish I had the guts
to tell you this is a place I hope
I never have to go through again.

Snake Sermon

In this picture you will see
Big Stone Gap, Virginia, the white
petals of dogwood blurred back
of the woman standing in what
we call the nave. She lifts
the snake, a moccasin, mouth pure
as cream when it opens, the shade
of Daddy's inner thigh. It ought
to be a rattler, big diamonds
chaining her throat like beads,
a tail to shake hell out of those
windows that overlook nothing.
But it's only black, thick
as horse cock in her little fingers,
its tongue licking the silence
out of the rough pews. You can't
buy rattlers anymore, big dozers
drove them away to prairies and
the snatching hands of farm boys
in sweat-belted baseball hats.
Times change, even way in here.
One cottonmouth per Sunday now,
bless the Lord for his bounty.
Three for Easter and Christmas.

Two Memories of a Rented House in a Southern State

1. With White Hair, They Come

And are always suddenly there, the knock on glass
polite, formal, a judge retired, teeth gold inlay.
Three raps, no more needed. The rest---

ful red flesh, wide-pored, lifted in the porch shade
as it was, doubtless, for her who came down the staircase
spiralling slowly. The black coat's threads

hang under the hanging white hair, a light grease
of sweat lies on the lip. The cane shuffles backward.
Recall of her name, and could you call please,

for someone is expected. That moment, again, awkward
if familiar, the red extended palm offering
confusion. Forced, you repeat, Sir, no card

lies in your hand, no one waits, there is nothing
to be done and, Sir, she has gone out under the willow.
Trembling now, white hair loose. The ring?

Someone is expected, there is a ring and, oh, you
see there was a misunderstanding, before
the hand retreats, the sun through magnolia

lays down a sizzling tunnel and he passes out where
in he came, in dust dazed and the leg, lame,
scratching like time. In the cool parlor

remember his drift back to the bench. Tenant, like him,
you will forget the sun, the dark, but the last
time you were loved always asks you in.

2. Young Woman, I Think I Know You

Or else he does not rise from the wicker chair
in which, in this memory, the eyes
glazed are pouring forth crystals, a river

you have seen but not walked in, white thighs
nakedly long in the sun, the first
hint of love leaping to his breath that sprays

as your skirt creeps up. You feel his hurt
glance follow you down the street
and the light is hot on him as passion or art.

If he should speak now? But he never quite does that.
In the same memory it is past dusk,
though the lemony memory is light and the heat

makes you kneel in cool dirt. Unearthing rust,
spoons orphaned early on, you pat
your hair as she did, the sweat on your breasts

tickling a little, and listen. Where he sits
most days the awning is curled in tight,
but the rocker rocks and there is no wind.

It could be a child. Children, like birds, fleet,
unexpected, who left, leaving the murmur
of movement you suddenly notice. It might

be he watches you again from a bed of shadows where
white-haired, sick, he calls her name
softly. Or else he has gone off combing his hair.

Because you are a woman whose heart, in pity, skids
you rise and go seek him out, but
not too fast, for he knows how a lady hides.

John Stone

He Makes a House Call

Six, seven years ago
when you began to faint
I painted your leg with iodine

threaded the artery
with the needle and then the tube
pumped your heart with dye enough

to see the valve
almost closed with stone.
We were both under pressure.

Today, in your garden,
kneeling under the sticky fig tree
for tomatoes

I keep remembering your blood.
Seven, it was. I was just
beginning to learn the heart

inside out.
Afterward, your surgery
and the precise valve of steel

and plastic that still pops and clicks
inside like a ping-pong ball.
I should try

chewing tobacco sometime
if only to see how it tastes.
There is a trace of it at the corner

of your leathery smile
which insists that I see inside
the house: someone named Bill I'm supposed

to know; the royal plastic soldier
whose body fills with whiskey
and marches on a music box

How Dry I Am;
the illuminated 3-D Christ who turns
into Mary from different angles;

the watery basement,
the pills you take, the ivy
that may grow around the ceiling

if it must. Here, you
are in charge—of figs, beans,
tomatoes, life.

At the hospital, a thousand times
I have heard your heart valve open, close.
I know how clumsy it is.

But health is whatever works
and for as long. I keep thinking
of seven years without a faint

on my way to the car
loaded, loaded with vegetables,
I keep thinking of seven years ago

when you bled in my hands like a saint.

Resuscitation

When the heart coughed
and the lungs folded
like flowers
your eyes had barely closed.

By all signs and proper science
you were dead

warm and dying
in one unmerciful
and unelectric instant.

Sweat hung
in my eyebrows
like a father's.

It is easier now
to reconstruct
your death in life.

How four days later
as you play at trains

I can remember
when the blood began
to bump like box-cars
in the back of your eyes.

Death

I have seen   come on
slowly as rust
sand

or suddenly   as when
someone leaving
a room

finds the doorknob
come loose in his hand

Dabney Stuart

The Ballad of the Volunteer

I could have tried to graduate
Or got a job instead,
Mother packed my underwear
Father held his head.

He never had a word for me
Or took the evening off,
Mother packed my hunting shirt
With the bloodstained cuff.

Rabbit and squirrel, and sometimes deer,
I made them dance a jig.
I'll get me in artillery
Where all the guns are big.

Where the guns are big in artillery
And the targets bigger still
I'll get me a bead on everything
I have to kill.

When the woods are close and the sun sinks
And a bird begins to call
There's not a thing moves on the earth
I won't teach to fall;

Everything that moves under the sun
Will wish me underground.
My mother packed my underwear.
He didn't make a sound.

The Soup Jar

Its metal top refused my father's twisting;
He tried warm water, a dishcloth, the heel of a shoe,
But couldn't budge its stubborn *status quo*.
It had stood its ground, longer than he, rusting.

I had to help. Gripped the jar while he cursed
Into place the tricky gadget guaranteed
To open anything, then gave it all he had.
I jerked my hand, and a hunk of glass, back when it burst.

Someone else tied my tourniquet. He paled
And had to sit down. Seven stitches later
We cleaned the floor and had another dish for supper.
Alone, he got nothing. It took us both to fail.

Weeks after, my world spun around that jar
And I saw it, and him, through angry tears.
Now it seems, recalled through these shattered years,
So small a thing—some broken glass, a scar.

Eleanor Ross Taylor

Victory

Granny Hill—no kin of course—said only sayings:
"Bad luck to drop your comb! Wind-storms come west . . .
"Bad luck to plant a cedar . . . it'll shade your grave."
Something forgotten, her face became obsessed;
She drew a cross-mark in her tracks,
Spat in the cross, before she would turn back.

The Saint girls mimicked her: Bad luck, bad luck!
"Come spend-the-night, girls—We'll eat boiled-butter-and-eggs."
Doctor Will, with a lantern, one fall night
Walked her orchard on dead legs,
And after that she had his power,
A remedy (some, though, severe)
For ingrown nails, chapped hands, consumption;
She talked fire from a swollen hand;
Was never sick herself.
Her face resided in a puckered bonnet;
Her clothes grew on her like a turtle's shell;
Bonnet and skirts smelled faintly henhouse.

Her Sally was a goose,
Shrill and dried up,
And where her baby came from no one knew
Unless it was George Jeans
Who drove the thresh.
But there was harmless Foolish John,
A man's beard, round black hat,
Round stomach like a two-year-old.
The Saint girls ran from him,
His grinning stare, the way he followed them.
He tore things up—old belts, old hats.
An old suspender was his favorite toy.
A moldy shoe found in the gully—Save it for John.
It was excitement,
Like George Jeans, the thresh, and chicken pie—
Three things he stabbed at saying,
Big-eyed, a prophet:
Geor' Jeans! Tresh? Chic' pie!

The Saint girls mimicked him,
Sometimes felt mimicked at the meeting house:
The turtleshell could say the Lord's Prayer backwards:
John sometimes said his words out loud,
Laughed, started for the pulpit.
A little screech from Sally brought him back.
"Whipping's all makes him learn," she'd wail.
They never saw him whipped or misbehave
(But taking off his clothes: "Like a baby—
Don't know no better.")

But one time he was lost three solid days.
Old Mr. Saint went out with them to search.
John! John-n-n!
They scoured the fields and woods all night
Carrying pine torches, calling,
(A lost dog would have come to whistling)
Stopping to stamp out broomstraw caught by sparks.
Three days, and gave him up.
Then found him under David Lee's cow-bridge,
Hovered, teeth chattering,
And led him home across the frozen fields.

Sunday he sat as empty as before.
Lord, whence are Thy hands so rent and torn?
They are pierc'd tonight by many a thorn!
Sally's high voice threw flames on the hymn;
The torches lit up Foolish John's pale face,
So much like hers, like Granny's—a pack of Hills—
And none of the ransom'd ever knew
How deep were the waters crossed
Or how dark the night the Lord passed through
Ere He found His sheep that was lost. . . .

John died first, of bloody flux;
Then Sally caught typhoid.
One morning Granny failed to wake.
Not dead, dried up and blown away, they thought.
Within a month Bess Saint at twilight
Appropriated Granny's shawl and bonnet,
Crept down from Granny's path to where the rest
Were picking berries. They threw their vessels

Far and wide, and to this day say, breathless,
"Bess, know that time—you dressed up like Granny?"

Woman as Artist

I'm mother.
I hunt alone.
There is no bone
Too dry for me, mother,
Or too extra.

Have a care, boy.
The neat pearls nibbling at the chowder
Gently, with joy,
Contain powder.

    An emigrant from the mother tongue
    To say-so in the silent one,
    For me the stepped-for step sinks,
    The expected light winks
    Out; dear self, do not think
    On the ominous appetite rising insistently
    In the hour of no food. . . .
    Do not think of the mice in the clock
    When you start up in your sleeping hood.
    The light feathers of a year,
    Too fine to make a pillow,
    Not fine enough to wear
    Out anywhere, drop but like milk
    Into the snow
    Of what I say and bear.

Kneel, fathers.
If my babies are right,
It is not because of you!
Or me.
But I lick them dearly,
Scrutinize their toilette,

Every tendril pleasing
On account of me. . . .

    Next year I'll dig them up
    And separate them.
    They'll multiply
      Multiply
        Multiply
    Till the round earth's ringed with Babel trumpets,
    Some dark, some light,
    Some streakèdy.

When I first gave the question life,
The howling naked question life,
Did I not have some inkling of the answer,
And the answer answered,
The door that closed across the room
As my door opened?

    In the morning, early,
    Birds flew over the stable,
    The morning glories ringed the flapping corn
    With Saturn faces for the surly light,
    And stars hung on the elder night.

    But in the afternoon
    Clouds came
    Cyclonic gusts and chilling rain
    Banged-to the windows of our heroine
    Beginning to chronicle her wound-up skein.
    Rib, spin.

Henry Taylor

Buildings and Grounds
FOR RICHARD DILLARD

The house we moved into has been landscaped
    so that it has the portable, plastic look
    of a Sears, Roebuck toy farm.

All up and down our street, the same minor artist seems
    to have been at work; our neighbors' lawns are
    watered and mowed truly until they are carpets,

their shrubs are lovingly trimmed and shaped
    into green velvet eggs and spheres.
    Our neighbors watch us like hawks,

wondering whether we have the equipment,
    the know-how, the spirit, to strive with them
    as they strive with their landscapes.

Oh, let me bring my home from the South to this street!
    I will let the grass grow until it is knee-high,

I will import chickens and a blue-tick hound to trample
    the grass and dig bone-holes and scratch-holes,

I will set up on cinderblocks in the front yard
    a '38 Ford with no tires or headlights,
    to shelter the hound and the chickens,

I will sit in the gutted driver's seat
    with a bottle of Old Mr. Mac, glaring at my
    neighbors, reading aloud from *God's Little Acre*,

I will be a prophet of wildness and sloth!

But the Puritan gaze of my neighbors cuts through
    my desperate vision of home—my dream house
    will not flourish here.

I will spend my rapidly declining years
    reading the labels on bags of crabgrass killer,

pushing my lawn mower until my front yard
    is as smooth as a green on a golf course,

clipping and shaping my landlord's opulent shrubs.

But don't misunderstand me—I have not been
     converted; I will still make something
     to sustain me here in this alien land.

I will plant mint in the flowerbeds beside
     the Shasta daisies we brought from Monticello,

I will set up a croquet course on the front lawn
     with a slender drink-stand at each wicket
     to hold my frosty mint juleps,

I will station an iron jockey by the driveway
     to stare back into the pitiless eyes
     of my neighbors' pink plastic flamingoes,

I will keep a Tennessee Walking Horse in the garage
     and give him a foxhound for company,

I will stand out front in a white linen suit
     surveying my plantation,

I will plant a magnolia tree.

But now, at the height of my visionary ecstasy,
     the telephone rings. It is the man
     next door, calling to let me know

that my sprinkler is turned up too high
     and is sprinkling the seats of his convertible.

I go out to turn down the water, and I see
     that the cedar needs trimming again,
     that the elm twigs need to be raked.

I will do those things. I will hoe and trench
     and weed, I will mow the grass.
     I have moved in here now,

and I have to do what I can.

Speech

1

I crouch over my radio
to tune in the President,
thinking how lucky I am
not to own a television.

2

Now the rich, cultivated voice
with its cautious, measured pauses
fills my living room, fills
the wastebasket, the vase
on the mantel, the hurricane
lamps, and even fills
the antique pottery whiskey jug
beside the fireplace, nourishing
the dried flowers I have put in it.

3

"I had a responsibility,"
he says; the phrase pours
from the speaker like molasses,
flows to the rug, spreads
into a black, shining puddle,
slowly expands, covers
the rug with dark sweetness.
It begins to draw flies;
they eat all the syrup
and clamor for more.

4

I can barely hear the speech
above the buzzing of their wings.
But the Commander in Chief
has the solution: another
phrase, sweeter, thicker,
blacker, oozes out
over my living room floor:

"I have personal reasons
for wanting peace." This is more
than the flies will be able to eat;
they will stay quiet
for the rest of the speech.

5

Now, you are thinking, comes
the Good Part, the part
where the syrup proves poisonous
and kills all the flies.
My fellow Americans, that
is not at all what happened.
The flies grew fat on the phrases,
grew as large as bullfrogs.

6

They are everywhere in the house,
and the syrup continues
to feed and fatten them;
in the pottery whiskey jug,
sprouting new leaves and buds,
even the dried flowers thrive.

7

The speech
has been over for weeks now;
they go on eating,
but they stay quiet
and seem peaceful enough.
At night, sometimes,
I can hear them
making soft liquid sounds
of contentment.

The Flying Change

1

The canter has two stride patterns, one on the right
lead and one on the left, each a mirror image of the
other. The leading foreleg is the last to touch the
ground before the moment of suspension in the air.
On cantered curves, the horse tends to lead with the
inside leg. Turning at liberty, he can change leads
without effort during the moment of suspension, but
a rider's weight makes this more difficult. The aim
of teaching a horse to move beneath you is to remind
him how he moved when he was free.

2

A single leaf turns sideways in the wind
in time to save a remnant of the day;
I am lifted like a whipcrack to the moves
I studied on that barbered stretch of ground,
before I schooled myself to drift away

from skills I still possess, but must outlive.
Sometimes when I cup water in my hands
and watch it slip away and disappear,
I see that age will make my hands a sieve;
but for a moment the shifting world suspends

its flight and leans toward the sun once more,
as if to interrupt its mindless plunge
through works and days that will not come again.
I hold myself immobile in bright air,
sustained in time astride the flying change.

William E. Taylor

I Must Come to Terms with Florida

If you have frost, poinsettias
die for Christmas.

June, with no December freeze,
is a fog of gnats.

You meet someone in the sun and look
through her body.

But this is all classical and I
must come to terms with my life.

Egrets are everywhere
studying egrets in white china water.

Scuba diving, I break off the tails
of lobsters, watching their heads float away.

I look up to see the sun
dissolving flake by flake into the sea.

A Woman Combing

Why should I wish to tell you who I am?
Words: if you look closely, the gull is ugly.
A scavenger and a bully, he loves crudely,
And he is, yes, restless, his eye always
On advantage. So, too, the pelican, but I
Can watch them skim the waves in formation
For hours and never think what swims beneath,
Nor of the basic, monotonous rhythms of the waves.
The gulls cry out of your mouth when the comb crackles,
And that is impatience and pain; you go to it then,
Laugh across the room as determined as the ocean.
Finally, the long glide and a kind of mistiness
Above it all, a motionlessness in motion,
And no one has spoken, no, not a word.

Ellen Bryant Voigt

Farm Wife

Dark as the spring river, the earth
opens each damp row as the farmer
swings the far side of the field.
The blackbirds flash their red
wing patches and wheel in his wake,
down to the black dirt; the windmill
grinds in its chain rig and tower.

In the kitchen, his wife is baking.
She stands in the door in her long white
gloves of flour. She cocks her head and
tries to remember, turns like the moon
toward the sea-black field. Her belly
is rising, her apron fills like a sail.
She is gliding now, the windmill churns
beneath her, she passes the farmer,
the fine map of the furrows.
The neighbors point to the bone-white
spot in the sky.

                    Let her float
like a fat gull that swoops and circles,
before her husband comes in for supper,
before her children grow up and leave her,
before the pulley cranks her down
the dark shaft, and the church blesses
her stone bed, and the earth seals
its black mouth like a scar.

Alice Walker

Burial

I

They have fenced in the dirt road
that once led to Wards Chapel
A.M.E. church,
and cows graze
among the stones that
mark my family's graves.
The massive oak is gone
from out the church yard,
but the giant space is left
unfilled;
despite the two-lane blacktop
that slides across
the old, unalterable
roots.

II

Today I bring my own child here;
to this place where my father's
grandmother rests undisturbed
beneath the Georgia sun,
above her the neatstepping hooves
of cattle.
Here the graves soon grow back into the land.
Have been known to sink. To drop open without
warning. To cover themselves with wild ivy,
blackberries. Bittersweet and sage.
No one knows why. No one asks.
When Burning Off Day comes, as it does
some years,
the graves are haphazardly cleared and snakes
hacked to death and burned sizzling
in the brush. . . . The odor of smoke, oak
leaves, honeysuckle.
Forgetful of geographic resolutions as birds,
the farflung young fly South to bury
the old dead.

III

The old women move quietly up
and touch Sis Rachel's face.
"Tell Jesus I'm coming," they say.
"Tell Him I ain't goin' to *be*
long."

My grandfather turns his creaking head
away from the lavender box.
He does not cry. But looks afraid.
For years he called her "Woman";
shortened over the decades to
"'Oman."
On the cut stone for "'Oman's" grave
he did not notice
they had misspelled her name.

(The stone reads *Racher Walker*—not "Rachel"—
Loving Wife, Devoted Mother.)

IV

As a young woman, who had known her? Tripping
eagerly, "loving wife," to my grandfather's
bed. Not pretty, but serviceable. A hard
worker, with rough, moist hands. Her own two
babies dead before she came.
Came to seven children.
To aprons and sweat.
Came to quiltmaking.
Came to canning and vegetable gardens
big as fields.
Came to fields to plow.
Cotton to chop.
Potatoes to dig.
Came to multiple measles, chickenpox,
and croup.
Came to water from springs.
Came to leaning houses one story high.
Came to rivalries. Saturday night battles.
Came to straightened hair, Noxzema, and
feet washing at the Hardshell Baptist church.

Came to zinnias around the woodpile.
Came to grandchildren not of her blood
whom she taught to dip snuff without
sneezing.
Came to death blank, forgetful of it all.

When he called her "'Oman" she no longer
listened. Or heard, or knew, or felt.

V

It is not until I see my first grade teacher
review her body that I cry.
Not for the dead, but for the gray in my
first grade teacher's hair. For memories
of before I was born, when teacher and
grandmother loved each other; and later
above the ducks made of soap and the orange-
legged chicks Miss Reynolds drew over
my own small hand
on paper with wide blue lines.

VI

Not for the dead, but for memories. None of
them sad. But seen from the angle of her
death.

Hymn

I well remember
A time when
"Amazing Grace" was
All the rage
In the South.
'Happy' black mothers arguing
Agreement with
Illiterate sweating preachers
Hemming and hawing blessedness

Meekness
Inheritance of earth, e.g.,
Mississippi cotton fields?

And in the North
Roy Hamilton singing
"What is America to me?"
Such a good question
From a nice slum
In North Philly.

My God! the songs and
The people and the lives
Started here—
Weaned on 'happy' tears
Black fingers clutching black teats
On black Baptist benches—
Some mother's troubles that everybody's
Seen
And nobody wants to see.

I can remember the rocking of
The church
And embarrassment
At my mother's shouts
Like it was all—'her happiness'—
Going to kill her.
My father's snores
Punctuating eulogies
His loud singing
Into fluffy grey caskets
A sleepy tear
In his eye.

Amazing Grace
How sweet the sound
That saved a wretch
Like me
I once was lost
But now I'm found
Was blind
But now
I see.

Mahalia Jackson, Clara Ward, Fats Waller,
Ray Charles,
Sitting here embarrassed with me
Watching the birth
Hearing the cries
Bearing witness
To the child,
Music.

James Whitehead

A Local Man Goes to the Killing Ground

They formed the ritual circle
    of Chevy trucks. Tracks were there,
    worn tires, the still prints in the mud
    and thin grass. My light could barely suggest
    the glare that fell on the men they killed.

It was an intimate thing—
    all of them drawn in so close
    they didn't bother with guns
    or the normal uses of the knife.
    It was done with boots.

I walked around that quiet place
    and tried to reclaim the energy
    that must of course remain in the earth.
    It keeps the truth to itself
    as they will, when they stride out of court.

By then it was all grey, false dawn—
    and I thought it was like stomping
    a fetus in the womb, a little
    skin between the killers, the killed,
    for the dead were curled in their passive way.

About a Year After He Got Married He Would Sit Alone in an Abandoned Shack in a Cotton Field Enjoying Himself

I'd sit inside the abandoned shack all morning
Being sensitive, a fair thing to do
At twenty-three, my first son born, and burning
To get my wife again. The world was new
And I was nervous and wonderfully depressed.

The light on the cotton flowers and the child
Asleep at home was marvelous and blessed,
And the dust in the abandoned air was mild

As sentimental poverty. I'd scan
Or draw the ragged wall the morning long.

Newspaper for wallpaper sang but didn't mean.
Hard thoughts of justice were beyond my ken.
Lord, forgive young men their gentle pain,
Then bring them stones. Bring their play to ruin.

Dara Wier

This Cold Nothing Else

A housesnake's made her nest in the woodshed.
Your man's gone again to a job.
He says it's south Florida where they build
all winter.

Milk fever makes you sleepy.
If the baby were weaned you'd work.
You've washed each window so they disappear
and it only lets in more weather.

Your one silver goblet shines on the sideboard
like a greedy mouth.
When you wear socks on the wood floor you slip down.
When you cook rice or grits
you hate the way the windows fog
and you feel buried inside.

Today like the wind the child won't quit crying.
When it cries again there's nothing to do
but scald it with milk until it stops.

Jonathan Williams

Dealer's Choice and the Dealer Shuffles
FOR WILLIAM BURROUGHS

I saw the Chattahoochee River get a haircut.
I saw Fidel Castro flow softly towards Apalachicola, Florida.

I saw a bank of red clay integrate with Jesuits.
I saw Bob Jones Bible University used to make baked flamingos.

I saw the Governor of Mississippi join the NAACP.
I saw a black gum tree refuse to leaf and go to jail.

I saw the DAR singing *"We Shall Overcome!"*
I saw Werner von Braun knitting gray (and brown) socks for the
    National Guard.

I saw the Motto of Alabama: "IT'S TOO WET TO PLOUGH!"
I saw God tell Adam: "WE DARE DEFEND OUR RIGHTS!"

I saw the City of Albany fried in deep fat.
I saw eight catfish star on Gomorrah TV.

I saw "THE INVASION OF THE BODY-SNATCHERS" at the Tyger
    Drive-In.
I saw William Blake grow like a virus in the sun.

I saw the South suckin hind titty.
I saw the North suckin hind titty.

I saw a man who saw these too
And said though strange they were all true.

The Ancient of Days

would that I
had known Aunt Cumi
Woody

C-u-m-i, pronounced
Q-my

she lived in the Deyton Bend Section of Mitchell
County, North Carolina many years ago

176

there is one of Bayard Wootten's photographs of her
standing there smiling with her store-bought
teeth, holding a coverlet

she sheared her sheep, spun
and dyed her yarn in vegetable dyes,
and wove the coverlet

in indigo, the brown from walnut roots,
red from madder, green from hickory ooze, first,
then into the indigo (the blue pot)

Cumi, from the Bible
(St. Mark 5:41)

Talitha Cumi:
Damsel, I say unto thee, arise!'

she is gone, she
enjoyed her days

The Priapupation of Queen Pasiphaë

say, lay
        off the doll biz, Daedalus,
construct me
            a stately mansion, dad, a conveyance
for my
        quote most monstrous lust unquote!

got just the rig, doll, try this
                    cow on—
for size . . .
o squeeze it, squeeze it, cool queen, it's ok, it's called
plywood—
            elastic and the latest!

ho! all's reet in Crete, daddio . . . so,
roll me over, into
the clover—
            thar whar that stud what's hung spiels

trash to them simple chicks,
                                    you dig?

man, mused Minos, so she's
a bitch on wheels . . .

moral:

white bulls, sacred to Poseidon,
don't fool
that easy, that's
for sure—

which is sort of
the first cock& bull story

for sure

Miller Williams

Getting Experience

The first real job I had was delivering drugs
for Jarman's Pharmacy in Bascum, Arkansas.

If everyone was busy or in the back I sold things.
A cloudy woman with pentecostal hair

softly asked for sanitary napkins.
She brought the Kleenex back unwrapped in twenty minutes.

Shame said Mr. Jordan. We shouldn't make a joke
of that and made me say I'm sorry and fired me.

When I found out what the woman wanted
I had to say I did what everyone said I did.

That or let them know I hadn't heard of Kotex.
Better be thought bad than known for stupid.

The first hard fight I had was after school
with Taylor Wardlow West in Bascum, Arkansas.

Ward West chased me home from school when I was lucky.
My father said Ward West was insecure.

Go smile at him he said and let him know
you mean to be his friend. My father believed in love.

All day I smiled and twisted in my seat to see him
all hate and slump by himself in the back of the room.

After school he sat on my chest and hit me
and then his little brother sat on my chest and hit me.

And then his little sister sat on my chest and hit me.
She made me so ashamed I tried to kick her

and kicked Ward West in the face. When he could see
I was rounding the corner for home. Jesus, Jesus, Jesus.

Next day everybody told me over and over
how I had balls to make those stupid faces,

him the son of a bitch of the whole school
and how I surely did kick the piss out of him.

Ward had to go to the dentist. Also his father beat him.
He didn't come to school for two days.

Then he left me alone. He said I was crazy.
Everybody thought I was a little crazy.

Although with balls. I just let them say I was.
Better be thought mad than known for stupid.

Sneeze, belch or fart. Choose if you have a choice.
Nobody's going to think you're good and sane and smart.

Why God Permits Evil:
For Answers to This Question
of Interest to Many
Write Bible Answers Dept. E-7
—AD ON A MATCHBOOK COVER

Of interest to John Calvin and Thomas Aquinas
for instance and Job for instance who never got

one straight answer but only his cattle back.
With interest, which is something, but certainly not

any kind of answer unless you ask
God if God can demonstrate God's power

and God's glory, which is not a question.
You should all be living at this hour.

You had Servetus to burn, the elect to count,
bad eyes and the Institutes to write;

You had the exercises and had Latin,
the hard bunk and the solitary night;

you had the neighbors to listen to and your woman
yelling at you to curse God and die.

Some of this to be on the right side;
some of it to ask in passing, Why?

Why badness makes its way in a world He made?
How come he looked for twelve and got eleven?

You had the faith and looked for love, stood pain,
learned patience and little else. We have E-7.

Churches may be shut down everywhere,
half-written philosophy books be tossed away.

Some place on the south side of Chicago
a lady with wrinkled hose and a small gray

bun of hair sits straight with her knees together
behind a teacher's desk on the third floor

of an old shirt factory, bankrupt and abandoned
except for this just cause, and on the door:

Dept. E-7. She opens the letters
asking why God permits it and sends a brown

plain envelope to each return address.
But she is not alone. All up and down

the thin and creaking corridors are doors
and desks behind them: E-6, E-5, 4, 3.

A desk for every question, for how we rise
blown up and burned, for how the will is free,

for when is Armageddon, for whether dogs
have souls or not and on and on. On

beyond the alphabet and possible numbers
where cross-legged, naked and alone,

there sits a tall and long-haired woman
upon a cushion of fleece and eiderdown

holding in one hand a hand-written answer,
holding in the other hand a brown

plain envelope. On either side, cobwebbed
and empty baskets sitting on the floor

say *in* and *out*. There is no sound in the room.
There is no knob on the door. Or there is no door.

Let Me Tell You

how to do it from the beginning.
First notice everything:
The stain on the wallpaper
of the vacant house,
the mothball smell of a
Greyhound toilet.
Miss nothing. Memorize it.
You cannot twist the fact you do not know.

Remember
The blonde girl you saw in the spade bar.
Put a scar on her breast.
Say she left home to get away from her father.
Invent whatever will support your line.
Leave out the rest.

Use metaphors: The mayor is a pig
is a metaphor
which is not to suggest
it is not a fact.
Which is irrelevant.
Nothing is less important
than a fact.

Be suspicious of any word you learned
and were proud of learning.
It will go bad.
It will fall off the page.
When your father lies
in the last light
and your mother cries for him,
listen to the sound of her crying.
When your father dies
take notes
somewhere inside.

If there is a heaven
he will forgive you
if the line you found was a good line.

It does not have to be worth the dying.

Charles Wright

Dog Creek Mainline

Dog Creek: cat track and bird splay,
Spindrift and windfall; woodrot;
Odor of muscadine, the blue creep
Of kingsnake and copperhead;
Nightweed; frog spit and floating heart,
Backwash and snag pool: Dog Creek

Starts in the leaf reach and shoal run of the blood;
Starts in the falling light just back
Of the fingertips; starts
Forever in the black throat
You ask redemption of, in wants
You waken to, the odd door:

Its sky, old empty valise,
Stands open, departure in mind; its three streets,
Y-shaped and brown,
Go up the hills like a fever;
Its houses link and deploy
—This ointment, false flesh in another color.

Five cutouts, five silhouettes
Against the American twilight; the year
Is 1941; remembered names
—Rosendale, Perry and Smith—
Rise like dust in the deaf air;
The tops spin, the poison swells in the arm:

The trees in their jade death-suits,
The birds with their opal feet,
Shimmer and weave on the shoreline;
The moths, like forget-me-nots, blow
Up from the earth, their wet teeth
Breaking the dark, the raw grain;

The lake in its cradle hums
The old songs: out of its ooze, their heads
Like tomahawks, the turtles ascend
And settle back, leaving their chill breath

In blisters along the bank;
Locked in their wide drawer, the pike lie still as knives.

Hard freight. It's hard freight
From Ducktown to Copper Hill, from Six
To Piled High: Dog Creek is on this line,
Indigent spur; cross-tie by cross-tie it takes
You back, the red wind
Caught at your neck like a prize:

(The heart is a hieroglyph;
The fingers, like praying mantises, poise
Over what they have once loved;
The ear, cold cave, is an absence,
Tapping its own thin wires;
The eye turns in on itself.

The tongue is a white water.
In its slick ceremonies the light
Gathers, and is refracted, and moves
Outward, over the lips,
Over the dry skin of the world.
The tongue is a white water.)

Northhanger Ridge

Half-bridge over nothingness,
White sky of the palette knife; blot orange,
Vertical blacks; blue, birdlike,
Drifting up from the next life,
The heat-waves, like consolation, wince—
One cloud, like a trunk, stays shut
Above the horizon; off to the left, dream-wires,
Hill-snout like a crocodile's.

Or so I remember it,
Their clenched teeth in their clenched mouths,
Their voices like shards of light,
Brittle, unnecessary.

Ruined shoes, roots, the cabinet of lost things:
This is the same story,
Its lips in flame, its throat a dark water,
The page stripped of its meaning.

Sunday, and Father Dog is turned loose:
Up the long road the children's feet
Snick in the dust like raindrops; the wind
Excuses itself and backs off; inside, heat
Lies like a hand on each head;
Slither and cough. Now Father Dog
Addles our misconceptions, points, preens,
His finger a white flag, run up, run down.

Bow-wow and arf, the Great Light;
O, and the Great Yes, and the Great No;
Redemption, the cold kiss of release,
&c.; sentences, sentences.
(Meanwhile docile as shadows, they stare
From their four corners, looks set:
No glitter escapes
This evangelical masonry.)

Candleflame; vigil and waterflow:
Like dust in the night the prayers rise:
From 6 to 6, under the sick Christ,
The children talk to the nothingness,
Crossrack and wound; the dark room
Burns like a coal, goes
Ash to the touch, ash to the tongue's tip;
Blood turns in the wheel:

Something drops from the leaves; the drugged moon
Twists and turns in its sheets; sweet breath
In a dry corner, the black widow reknits her dream.
Salvation again declines,
And sleeps like a skull in the hard ground,
Nothing for ears, nothing for eyes;
It sleeps as it's always slept, without
Shadow, waiting for nothing.

Blackwater Mountain

That time of evening, weightless and disparate,
When the loon cries, when the small bass
Jostle the lake's reflections, when
The green of the oak begins
To open its robes to the dark, the green
Of water to offer itself to the flames,
When lily and lily pad
Husband the last light
Which flares like a white disease, then disappears:
This is what I remember. And this:

The slap of the jacklight on the cove;
The freeze-frame of ducks
Below us; your shots; the wounded flop
And skid of one bird to the thick brush;
The moon of your face in the fire's glow;
The cold; the darkness. Young,
Wanting approval, what else could I do?
And did, for two hours, waist-deep in the lake,
The thicket as black as death,
Without success or reprieve, try.

The stars over Blackwater Mountain
Still dangle and flash like hooks, and ducks
Coast on the evening water;
The foliage is like applause.
I stand where we stood before and aim
My flashlight down to the lake. A black duck
Explodes to my right, hangs, and is gone.
He shows me the way to you;
He shows me the way to a different fire
Where you, black moon, warm your hands.

Depression Before the Solstice

4 days till the solstice, the moon
Like an onion thin in the afternoon sky, the few leaves
In the liquidambar arthritic and holding on.
The weightless, unclarified light from the setting sun
Lies like despair on the ginger root. Windows
Go up in flame. Now

The watchers and holy ones set out, divining
The seal, eclipses
Taped to their sleeves like black felt,
Their footprints filling with sparks
In the bitter loam behind them, ahead of them stobbed with sand,
And walk hard, and regret nothing.

Al Young

A Dance for Ma Rainey

I'm going to be just like you, Ma
Rainey this monday morning
clouds puffing up out of my head
like those balloons
that float above the faces of white people
in the funnypapers

I'm going to hover in the corners
of the world, Ma
& sing from the bottom of hell
up to the tops of high heaven
& send out scratchless waves of yellow
& brown& that basic black honey
misery

I'm going to cry so sweet
& so low
& so dangerous,
Ma,
that the message is going to reach you
back in 1922
where you shimmer
snaggle-toothed
perfumed&
powdered
in your bauble beads
hair pressed& tied back
throbbing with that sick pain
I know
& hide so well
that pain that blues
jives the world with
aching to be heard
that downness
that bottomlessness
first felt by some stolen delta nigger
swamped under with redblooded american agony;
reduced to the sheer shit
of existence

that bred
& battered us all,
Ma,
the beautiful people
our beautiful brave black people
who no longer need to jazz
or sing to themselves in murderous vibrations
or play the veins of their strong tender arms
with needles
to prove that we're still here

A Dance for Militant Dilettantes

No one's going to read
or take you seriously,
a hip friend advises,
until you start coming down on them
like the black poet you truly are
& ink in lots of black in your poems
soul is not enough
you need real color
shining out of real skin
nappy snaggly afro hair
baby grow up & dig on *that*!

You got to learn to put in about
stone black fists
coming up against white jaws
& red blood splashing
down those fabled wine & urine-
stained hallways
black bombs blasting out real white estate
the sky itself black with what's to come:
final holocaust
the settling up

Dont nobody want no nice nigger no more
these honkies man that put out

these books & things
they want an angry splib

a furious nigrah
they dont want no bourgeois woogie
they want them a militant nigger
in a fiji haircut
fresh out of some secret boot camp
with a bad book in one hand
& a molotov cocktail in the other
subject to turn up at one of their conferences
or soirees
& shake the shit out of them

Birthday Poem

First light of day in Mississippi
son of laborer & of house wife
it says so on the official photostat
not son of fisherman & child fugitive
from cottonfields & potato patches
from sugarcane chickens & well-water
from kerosene lamps & watermelons
mules named jack or jenny & wagonwheels,

years of meaningless farm work
work Work WORK WORK WORK—
"Papa pull you outta school bout March
to stay on the place & work the crop"
—her own earliest knowledge
of human hopelessness & waste

She carried me around nine months
inside her fifteen year old self
before here I sit numbering it all

How I got from then to now
is the mystery that could fill a whole library
much less an arbitrary stanza

But of course you already know about that
from your own random suffering
& sudden inexplicable bliss

Pachuta, Mississippi / A Memoir

I too
once lived
in the country

    Incandescent
      fruits
    in moonlight
    whispered to me
      from trees
      of
  1950
swishing
  in the green nights

      wavelengths away
        from
      tongue-red meat
      of melon

      wounded squash
    yellow as old afternoons

    chicken
      in love
        with calico
            hiss & click of flit gun

        juice music
        you suck up
      lean stalks of field cane

            Cool as sundown
            I lived there too

BETTY ADCOCK was born in San Augustine, Texas, in 1938. She graduated from Hockaday School and later attended four different colleges and universities. Her career as a writer began after she married and moved to Raleigh, North Carolina, where she now works as a copywriter for an advertising agency. She has been an editor of *Southern Poetry Review*, worked in the Poetry-in-the-Schools program, and taught creative writing at Duke University. Her poems have appeared in *Poetry Southwest, Nation*, and other national publications, and her first book, *Wallking Out*, was published by LSU Press in 1976.

A. R. AMMONS was born in Whiteville, North Carolina, in 1926. He graduated from Wake Forest College and later attended the University of California at Berkeley. He lived for a year on the Outer Banks of North Carolina's coast, where he was principal of Hatteras Elementary School. Later he was a business executive in New Jersey, but since 1964 he has taught at Cornell University. His *Collected Poems: 1951–1971* was chosen for the National Book Award in 1972; he has also won the Levinson Prize and the Bollingen Prize. Some of his recent books are *Diversifications, Sphere: The Form of a Motion*, and *The Snow Poems*.

JAMES APPLEWHITE was born in Stantonsburg, North Carolina, in 1935, and grew up on a tobacco farm in Wilson County. He has taught at the University of North Carolina at Greensboro and is now teaching creative writing at Duke University, where he earned his B.A., M.A., and Ph.D. degrees. His poems have been published in *Shenandoah, New American Review, Poetry, Harper's, Young American Poets*, and other journals and anthologies. His first book of poems, *Statues of the Grass*, was published in 1975, and he is also the editor of a collection of writings on the environment, *Voices from Earth*.

ALVIN AUBERT was born in Lutcher, Louisiana, on March 12, 1930. He earned his B.A. from Southern University at Baton Rouge and his M.A. from the University of Michigan in 1960. Now associate professor of English at the State University of New York, Fredonia, he was a faculty member at Southern University from 1960–1970. He is editor of *Obsidian* and has been a recipient of a National Endowment for the Arts grant and a Bread Loaf Fellowship. His first collection of poems, *Against the Blues*, was published in 1972; his second, *Feeling Through*, in 1975.

COLEMAN BARKS was born in Chattanooga, Tennessee, in 1937. His B.A. and Ph.D. degrees are from the University of North Carolina at Chapel Hill, and his M.A. from the University of California at Berkeley. Now teaching at the University of Georgia, he has also taught at the Universities of North Carolina and Southern California. His poems have appeared in *Chelsea, Red Clay Reader, Tennessee Poetry Journal, Carolina Quarterly, Fiddlehead*, and several anthologies. His first collection, *The Juice*, was published by Harper & Row in 1972. Two recent chapbooks are *New Words* and *We're Laughing at the Damage*.

GERALD BARRAX, who teaches black studies and creative writing at North Carolina State University, was born in Alabama in 1933. He has a B.A. degree from Duquesne University and an M.A. from the University of Pittsburgh. In addition to teaching, he has worked as a steelmill laborer, cab driver, and mail carrier. His poems have appeared in *Poetry*, *Southern Poetry Review*, and numerous journals and anthologies of black writers. His first collection, *Another Kind of Rain*, was published in 1970 by the University of Pittsburgh Press.

JOHN BEECHER was born in 1904 in New York City, but has lived much of his life in the South. He earned his B.A. from the University of Alabama and an M.A. from the University of Wisconsin; he also studied at several other universities, including the Univesity of North Carolina at Chapel Hill. Now retired and living in Burnsville, North Carolina, he has taught English and sociology and been poet-in-residence at a number of universities and colleges, among them Duke University. In addition, he has held a variety of jobs, including work as a steel worker, government administrator, and journalist. Known as a poet of protest, he has published over twenty books, culminating in *Collected Poems, 1924–1974*, published by Macmillan.

D. C. BERRY was born in 1942 in Vicksburg, Mississippi. He holds the B.S. degree in mathematics from Bob Jones University, a B.S. in biology from Delta State College, and a Ph.D. in English from the University of Tennessee. He has taught at the University of Tennessee and is currently a member of the faculty of the University of Southern Mississippi, where he is poetry editor of the *Mississippi Review*. Widely published in magazines and anthologies, he has also published a collection of poems, *Saigon Cemetery*, which is based on his experiences in Vietnam.

WENDELL BERRY was born in Henry County, Kentucky, on August 5, 1934. He earned his A.B. and M.A. degrees from the University of Kentucky, where he has taught creative writing since 1954. He has been a recipient of Guggenheim and Rockefeller Fellowships and a National Endowment for the Arts grant. He has published three novels and several collections of essays, in addition to six volumes of poetry, which include *The Broken Ground*, *Farming: A Hand Book*, *Openings*, and *Findings*.

HELEN BEVINGTON, born in 1906, grew up in upper New York State; however, her active career began when her husband joined the faculty at Duke University. She has lived in Durham, North Carolina, since 1943, where she taught in the English Department at Duke University until her recent retirement. She holds a Ph.D. from the University of Chicago and an M.A. from Columbia University. Among her popular collections of light verse are *Doctor Johnson's Waterfall*, *A Change of Sky*, *When Found, Make Verse Of*, and *Beautiful, Lofty People*.

DAVID BOTTOMS was born in Canton, Georgia, in 1949. He has a B.A. from Mercer University and an M.A. from West Georgia College. Formerly editor of *The Dulcimer* and *Eclectic*, he currently edits the Burnt Hickory Press series. His poems have been published in *Harper's*, *Prairie Schooner*, *Southern Poetry Review*, and other literary magazines. He has also published a chapbook, *Jamming with the Band at the VFW*, 1978, and was the 1979 winner of the Walt Whitman Award.

EDGAR BOWERS was born in Rome, Georgia, on March 2, 1924. His B.A. is from the University of North Carolina at Chapel Hill and his M.A. and Ph.D. degrees are from Stanford University. He taught at Duke University and Harpur College, New York, and he is now professor of English at the University of California, Santa Barbara, where he has been on the faculty since 1958. He has been awarded a Guggenheim Fellowship and a Fulbright Fellowship. Among his collections of poetry are *The Form of Loss*, *The Astronomers*, *Living Together: New and Selected Poems*, and *Paroxisms: A Guide to the Isms*.

JOHN BRICUTH (JOHN IRWIN) was born in 1940 in Houston, Texas. After graduating from the University of St. Thomas in Houston, he took his M.A. and Ph.D. degrees at Rice University. Following military service in the Navy, he worked at NASA as supervisor of the Public Affairs Library. He taught at the Bread Loaf School of English, Middlebury College, and then at Johns Hopkins University, where he is now chairman of the Department of Contemporary Writing. He has also edited *Striver's Row* and *Georgia Review*. His collection of poems, *The Heisenberg Variations*, was published in 1976 by the University of Georgia Press.

BESMILR BRIGHAM, who is part Choctaw, was born in Pace, Mississippi, in 1923. She studied at the New School for Social Research, and now lives on a farm in Horatio, Arkansas. In 1970 she received a National Endowment for the Arts grant. Her poems have appeared in *Southern Review* and other literary journals, and she has also published a number of short stories. Her two collections of poetry are *Heaved from the Earth* and *Agony Dance: Death of the Dancing Dolls*.

VAN K. BROCK was born in 1932 and grew up on a farm near Moultrie, Georgia. He was educated at Emory University and the University of Iowa, where he earned M.A., M.F.A., and Ph.D. degrees. Since 1970 he has taught at Florida State University in Tallahassee. For over a decade his work has appeared in such journals as *Yale Review*, *North American Review*, *Prairie Schooner*, and *Shenandoah*. In 1977 and 1978 two chapbooks of his poems were published, *Weighing the Penalties* and *Spelunking*.

TURNER CASSITY was born in 1929 in Jackson, Mississippi. He earned a B.A. at Millsaps College, an M.A. at Stanford University, and (following military service) an M.S. at Columbia University. A librarian, he has held positions in libraries in Jackson, Mississippi, and Pretoria, South Africa, and since 1962 in the Emory University Library in Atlanta. His books include *Watchboy, What of the Night?* in the Wesleyan poetry series and *Steeplejacks in Babel* from Godine.

FRED CHAPPELL was born in Canton, North Carolina, in 1936. He received both his B.A. and M.A. degrees from Duke University, where he studied under the late William Blackburn. Now living in Greensboro, he is professor of English at the University of North Carolina at Greensboro, where he teaches creative writing and modern fiction. In addition to poetry, he has published four novels and numerous short stories. His collections of poems, published by LSU Press, are *The World Between the Eyes*, *River*, and *Bloodfire*.

JOHN WILLIAM CORRINGTON was born in 1932 in Memphis, Tennessee. After graduating from Centenary College in Shreveport, Louisiana, he took his M.A. at Rice University and his Ph.D. at the University of Sussex. He also holds a law degree from Tulane University. A recipient of a National Endowment for the Arts grant, he has taught at Louisiana State University and Loyola University in New Orleans; he has also practiced law. In addition to writing screen plays, he has published three novels and a collection of short stories as well as four volumes of verse, including *Where We Are, Mr. Clean and Other Poems*, and *Lines to the South and Other Poems*. With Miller Williams he co-edited *Southern Writing in the Sixties: Fiction* and *Southern Writing in the Sixties: Poetry*.

ROSEMARY DANIELL was born in Georgia in 1935. She has been a freelance journalist, ad agency creative director, teacher of poetry workshops, and director of Georgia's Poetry-in-the-Schools program. Her poems have appeared in *Atlantic Monthly, Great Speckled Bird, Southern Poetry Review*, and other magazines. In 1975 Doubleday published her first book of poems, *A Sexual Tour of the Deep South*; it was followed by *The Feathered Trees* from Sweetwater Press. She is currently at work on a new collection of poems and a book on southern women.

ANN DEAGON was born in 1930 in Birmingham, Alabama. She graduated from Birmingham Southern College in 1950 and received an M.A. and Ph.D. in classics from the University of North Carolina at Chapel Hill. She now lives in Greensboro and teaches at Guilford College. Although she did not start writing seriously until she was forty, nearly two hundred of her poems have been published in over fifty different magazines and anthologies. She has published five books of poetry, including *Poetics South, Carbon 14*, and *There is No Balm in Birmingham*. Recently she has also turned to writing fiction.

JAMES DICKEY was born in Atlanta, Georgia, in 1923. He attended Clemson College and Vanderbilt University, where he earned his B.A. and M.A. degrees. He taught at several universities and served as consultant in poetry at the Library of Congress before becoming professor of English and writer-in-residence at the University of South Carolina, where he has been since 1969. He has received the National Book Award for *Poems: 1957–1967*, a Guggenheim Fellowship, and a National Institute of Arts and Letters grant. He has published eight collections of poetry, a novel, *Deliverance*, and several critical works. His latest volumes of poetry are *The Eye-Beaters, Blood, Victory, Madness, Buckhead and Mercy*, and *Zodiac*.

R. H. W. DILLARD was born in Roanoke, Virginia, in 1937. After graduating from Roanoke College, he earned his M.A. and Ph.D. degrees from the University of Virginia and is now professor of English at Hollins College, Virginia, where he teaches creative writing and is on the staff of the *Hollins Critic*. He has received a Ford grant and an Academy of American Poets Prize. In addition to a novel and a play, he has published three books of poetry: *The Day I Stopped Dreaming About Barbara Steele and Other Poems* and *News of the Nile* from the University of North Carolina Press and *After Borges* from LSU Press.

CHARLES EDWARD EATON was born in Winston-Salem, North Carolina, in 1916. He attended Duke University, the University of North Carolina at Chapel Hill, Princeton University, and Harvard University, where he received his M.A. He has taught in Puerto Rico, at the University of Missouri, and at the University of North Carolina at Chapel Hill, and has also served as vice-consul of the American Embassy in Rio de Janeiro. Since 1951 he has been a free-lance writer and art critic. He is the author of a book of art criticism, six books of poetry, a play, and two volumes of short stories. He has won several awards, including the Alice Fay di Castagnola Award for *The Man in the Green Chair* and the Roanoke-Chowan Award for *On the Edge of the Knife*.

GEORGE GARRETT was born in 1929 in Orlando, Florida. He holds B.A. and M.A. degrees from Princeton University and also studied at Columbia University. He has taught and served as writer-in-residence at several universities, including Princeton University, the University of Virginia, Hollins College, and the University of South Carolina. He has received a Ford grant, a Guggenheim Fellowship, and a National Endowment for the Arts grant. Editor of numerous books and magazines, he has published five novels, four collections of short stories, and two plays. Among his four collections of verse, the most recent is *For a Bitter Season: New and Selected Poems*.

ANDREW GLAZE was born in 1920 in Birmingham, Alabama, though he has lived for the past two decades in New York. He graduated from Harvard University and served as an officer with the U.S. Army Air Corps during World War II. His poems have appeared frequently in the *New Yorker* and *Poetry*, and he has published two collections of poetry, *Damned Ugly Children* and *A Masque of Surgery*. He has won the Eunice Tietjens Award for poetry.

JAMES BAKER HALL was born in Lexington, Kentucky, in 1935, and educated at the University of Kentucky and Stanford University, where he held a Wallace Stegner Writing Fellowship in 1960–1961. He has taught at Massachusetts Institute of Technology, New York University, and the University of Kentucky, where he is currently director of creative writing. He has also taught photography and published widely as a photographer. Among his publications are two novels and a chapbook of poems, *Getting It on up to the Brag*, 1975.

WILLIAM HARMON was born in Concord, North Carolina, in 1938. After earning his B.A. at the University of Chicago, he served in the Navy and spent seven years on active duty assigned to a destroyer. In 1970, after receiving his Ph.D. from the University of Cincinnati, he returned to his native state to teach at the University of North Carolina, where he served six years as chairman of the English Department. In addition to writing a book on Ezra Pound and editing *The Oxford Book of American Light Verse*, he has published three collections of poetry: *Treasury Holiday, Legion: Civic Choruses*, and *The Intussusception of Miss Mary America*.

DONALD JUSTICE was born in Miami, Florida, in 1925. He received his B.A. from the University of Miami, his M.A. from the University of North Carolina at Chapel Hill, and his Ph.D. from the University of Iowa, where he has taught for over two decades. He has been a recipient of a National Endowment for the Arts grant, a Ford Fellowship, and a National Institute of Arts and Letters Award. He has edited four books and published several volumes of poetry, including *The Summer Anniversaries, Night Light, Departures,* and *Selected Poems.*

DAVID KIRBY was born in Baton Rouge, Louisiana, in 1944. He earned a B.A. degree from Louisiana State University and a Ph.D. from Johns Hopkins University. Since 1969 he has been on the faculty of Florida State University, where he directs the writing program. His poems have appeared in *Southern Poetry Review, South Carolina Review,* and other literary journals. He is the author of a chapbook of poems entitled *The Opera Lover.*

ETHERIDGE KNIGHT was born in 1931 in Corinth, Mississippi, where he was educated in the public schools. He has been poet-in-residence at the University of Pittsburgh, Hartford University, and Lincoln University. He has also served as editor of *Motive* (Nashville, Tenn.) and *Black Box* (Washington, D.C.). He has received a National Endowment for the Arts grant and a Guggenheim Fellowship. Among his six volumes of verse are *Poems from Prison, A Poem for Brother Man,* and *Belly Song and Other Poems.*

DUANE LOCKE was born in Vienna, Georgia, in 1921. He earned a Ph.D. at the University of Florida and is now poet-in-residence at the University of Tampa, where he edits *Poetry Review.* A prolific writer and editor, he has been published in more than 250 magazines. He is the founder of the Immanentist Movement, dedicated to poetry based on the superconscious, which, Locke says, seeks "a heightened awareness . . . by cleansing the conventional from the senses and overcoming the estrangement from animals, vegetables, and minerals." Among his books are *From the Bottom of the Sea, Dead Cities,* and *Rainbow Under Boards.*

JEFF DANIEL MARION was born in 1940 in Rogersville, Tennessee, and received his B.S. and M.A. in English from the University of Tennessee at Knoxville. He now lives in Jefferson City, where he edits *The Small Farm.* He is associate professor of English at Carson-Newman College and teaches creative writing and contemporary poetry. He is the author of two chapbooks of poetry and *Out in the Country, Back Home,* 1976.

JIM WAYNE MILLER was born in Leicester, North Carolina, and grew up in the North Carolina mountains. He has a B.A. from Berea College and a Ph.D. in German and American literature from Vanderbilt University. He teaches in the language department at Western Kentucky University at Bowling Green. His poems have been published in many journals, and his two books of poetry are *Copper Head Cane* and *Dialogue with a Dead Man.*

VASSAR MILLER was born in Houston, Texas, in 1924. She received her B.A. and M.A. degrees from the University of Houston and has taught at St. John's

School there. Her five volumes of poetry are *Adam's Footprint, Wage War on Silence, My Bones Being Wiser, Onions and Roses,* and *If I Could Sleep Deeply Enough.* Her chapbook *Small Change* was published in 1976.

WILLIAM MILLS was born in Hattiesburg, Mississippi, and reared in Louisiana. He holds a Ph.D. from Louisiana State University and a diploma from Goethe Institute, Blaubeuren, Germany. While in the Army he lived in Kyoto, Japan. He has taught at several universities in the South, including the University of Arkansas. He has published two collections of poetry, *Watch for the Fox* and *Stained Glass* from LSU Press, as well as a book of fiction and a critical study of Howard Nemerov.

MARION MONTGOMERY was born in Upson County, Georgia, in 1925, and holds the A.B. and M.A. degrees from the University of Georgia. He has been business manager of *Georgia Review* and assistant director of the University of Georgia Press. Montgomery has taught for twenty years at the University of Georgia, where he is now professor of English. He has published three novels and several books of criticism, including *Ezra Pound: A Critical Essay.* His three volumes of poetry are *Dry Lightning, Stones from the Rubble,* and *The Gull and Other Georgia Scenes.*

ROBERT MORGAN was born in Hendersonville, North Carolina, in 1944, and lived in Zirconia, North Carolina, from 1944 until 1961. After attending North Carolina State University, he graduated from the University of North Carolina at Chapel Hill in 1965 and later received his M.F.A. from the University of North Carolina at Greensboro. At present he is teaching creative writing at Cornell University. He is the author of three volumes of poetry: *Zirconia Poems, Red Owl,* and *Land Diving.*

PAUL BAKER NEWMAN was born in 1919 and grew up in Chicago, though most of his writing has been done in the South. He has an M.F.A. from the Writers Workshop at the University of Iowa and a Ph.D. from the University of Chicago. He has taught at Manhattan, Kansas, worked as a weather forecaster, and served five years in the Army during World War II. He is living now in Charlotte, North Carolina, where he teaches creative writing at Queens College. Among his five books are *The Cheetah and the Fountain, The Ladder of Love,* and *The House on the Saco.*

SAM RAGAN was born in Berea, North Carolina, in 1915. After graduating from Atlantic Christian College in Wilson, North Carolina, he embarked on a career in journalism. He has also been a TV commentator and moderator, critic, editor, and teacher of writing workshops. Currently he lives in Southern Pines, North Carolina, where he edits and publishes *The Pilot.* In addition to three books of nonfiction, he has published two collections of poetry. *The Tree in the Far Pasture* and *To the Water's Edge.*

PAUL RAMSEY, born in Atlanta in 1924, received his B.A. and M.A. degrees from the University of North Carolina at Chapel Hill and his Ph.D. from the

University of Minnesota. Currently professor of English and poet-in-residence at the University of Tennessee at Chattanooga, he has also taught at the University of Alabama, Elmira College in New York, and the University of the South in Tennessee. Among his awards are the SAMLA Studies Award in 1968 for *The Art of John Dryden*. His collections of poetry include *In an Ordinary Place, Triptych*, and *No Running on the Boardwalk*.

JULIA RANDALL was born in Baltimore, Maryland, in 1923. She received her B.A. from Bennington College and M.A. from Johns Hopkins University. From 1952–1954 she lived in Paris. She taught at Hollins College, Virginia, for over a decade, but she is now retired and living in Glen Arm, Maryland. She has received both a National Endowment for the Arts grant and a National Institute of Arts and Letters grant. Among her six collections of poems are *The Solstice Tree, The Puritan Carpenter*, and *Adam's Dream*.

GIBBONS RUARK was born in Raleigh, North Carolina, in 1941, and educated at the University of North Carolina at Chapel Hill and the University of Massachusetts, where he received his M.A. After teaching at the University of North Carolina at Greensboro, he joined the faculty at the University of Delaware as a teacher of creative writing. His poems have appeared in the *New Yorker, Poetry*, and *Southern Poetry Review*; and he has published two books, *A Program for Survival* and *Reeds*.

LARRY RUBIN was born in 1930 in Bayonne, New Jersey, and grew up in Miami Beach, Florida. He holds the B.A., M.A., and Ph.D. degrees from Emory University. At present he is professor of English at Georgia Institute of Technology, where he has taught since 1956. He has also taught in Poland, Norway, Germany, and Austria as a Fulbright lecturer in American literature. His collections of poetry are *The World's Old Way, Lanced in Light*, and *All My Mirrors Lie*.

SONIA SANCHEZ was born in Birmingham, Alabama, in 1934, and earned her B.A. at Hunter College. She has taught at several colleges, including Rutgers University, Amherst College, the University of Pennsylvania, and Temple University, where she is now an associate professor. One of the best-known black poets, she has read her poetry at more than two hundred colleges, and her poems have been widely anthologized. She has published five plays, two children's books, and seven volumes of poetry, including *WE a BaddDDD People, A Blues Book for Blue Black Magical Women, Love Poems*, and *Haiku(s), Tanka(s) and Other Love Syllables*.

GEORGE SCARBROUGH was born in Patty, Tennessee, in 1915, and makes his home now in Oak Ridge. He attended a number of colleges, including the University of Tennessee, the University of the South, and the University of Iowa. In addition to farming and doing newspaper work, he taught English and writing in public schools and a junior college for eighteen years. Recipient of two Carnegie Foundations grants, he also received a Borestone Mountain Award in

1961. Among his books are *The Course Is Upward, Summer So-Called*, and *New and Selected Poems*, published by Iris Press in 1977.

JAMES SEAY was born in 1939 in Panola County, Mississippi. After graduating from the University of Missippi, he took his M.A. at the University of Virginia in 1966. He now teaches at the University of North Carolina at Chapel Hill. His poems have appeared in numerous magazines, including *American Review* and *Nation*. His two collections of poetry, *Let Not Your Hart* and *Water Tables*, were published in the Wesleyan poetry series.

EDGAR SIMMONS was born in 1921 in Natchez, Mississippi, and grew up in the Deep South. He received two degrees in English at Columbia University and studied at the Sorbonne in Paris. In addition to working as a newspaper editor, he has taught English and creative writing at DePauw University, William and Mary, Mississippi College, and the University of Texas at El Paso. Simmons has received the Texas Institute of Letters Award and the Henry Bellamann Literary Award for poetry. He is currently a free-lance writer living in Jackson, Mississippi. His two volumes of poetry are *Pocahontas and Other Poems* and *Driving to Biloxi*.

DAVE SMITH was born in Portsmouth, Virginia, in 1942. He has a B.A. from the University of Virginia and an M.A. and Ph.D. from Southern Illinois University. He spent four years in the United States Air Force, and has been a high school football coach, bartender, and teacher. Formerly editor of *Back Door*, he is currently teaching creative writing at the University of Utah. He has published several volumes of poetry, including *Mean Rufus Throw Down, The Fisherman's Whore*, and *Cumberland Station*.

JOHN STONE was born in Jackson Mississippi, in 1936. He holds a B.A. degree from Millsaps College and an M.D. degree from Washington University School of Medicine. He is now professor of medicine at Emory University School of Medicine and director of emergency medicine residency at Grady Memorial Hospital in Atlanta. His poems have appeared in many magazines and anthologies, and he has published a collection, *The Smell of Matches*, Rutgers University Press.

DABNEY STUART was born in 1937 in Richmond, Virginia, where he attended the public schools. After graduating from Davidson College, he earned his M.A. in English at Harvard University. For a number of years he was poetry editor of *Shenandoah* and taught at Washington and Lee University. He has also taught at the College of William and Mary. His books of verse include *The Diving Bell, A Particular Place, The Other Hand*, and *Round and Round: A Triptych*.

ELEANOR ROSS TAYLOR was born in North Carolina in 1920. She was graduated from the University of North Carolina at Greensboro (then Woman's College) and in 1943 was married to Peter Taylor, the writer. For some years she has lived in Charlottesville, Virginia. She has published two collections of poems, *Wilderness of Ladies* and *Welcome Eumenides*, and she also writes short stores.

HENRY TAYLOR, born in Virginia in 1942, earned a B.A. from the University of Virginia and an M.A. in creative writing from Hollins College. He has taught at Roanoke College, University of Utah, and American University, where he is currently associate professor of English. He has published three collections of poems: *The Horse Show at Midnight*, *Breakings*, and *An Afternoon of Pocket Billiards*.

WILLIAM E. TAYLOR was born in Newark, New Jersey, but his writing career has been spent in the South. After attending Columbia University, he received his B.A., M.A., and Ph.D. degrees from Vanderbilt University. Since 1957 he has taught at Stetson University, where he is chairman of the Department of English. In addition to editing a poetry magazine for nearly a decade, he has published a number of chapbooks. Among those that make special use of Florida as a setting are *Down Here with Aphrodite* and *Devoirs to Florida*.

ELLEN BRYANT VOIGT was born in Virginia in 1943 and grew up there. She was educated at Converse College in South Carolina and the Writers Workshop at the University of Iowa. Currently she lives in Cabot, Vermont, and directs the M.F.A. writing program at Goddard College. Her poems have appeared in *Sewanee Review*, *Nation*, and *Southern Review*, as well as other journals. Her first collection of poems, *Claiming Kin*, is in the Wesleyan series.

ALICE WALKER was born in 1944 in Eatontown, Georgia. She attended Spelman College and was graduated from Sarah Lawrence College. Currently she is a fiction editor of *Ms.* magazine, an editor of a periodical of the black freedom movement, *Freedomways*, and a teacher of fiction at Yale. She has received numerous awards and fellowships, including the Lillian Smith Award, a National Endowment for the Arts Award, and a Radcliffe Institute Fellowship. Best known as a novelist, she has written short stories, essays, biography, and poetry. Her poetry collections are *Once* and *Revolutionary Petunias*.

JAMES WHITEHEAD was born in 1936 in St. Louis, Missouri, and grew up in Mississippi. He earned his B.A. and M.A. degrees at Vanderbilt University, and an M.F.A. at the University of Iowa. He has taught at Millsaps College in Mississippi and is now associate professor of English at the University of Arkansas, where he teaches creative writing. He received a Guggenheim grant in 1972 and the Bread Loaf Writers Conference Robert Frost Fellowship in 1967. He has published a novel, *Joiner*, and a collection of poems, *Domains*.

DARA WIER was born in 1949 in New Orleans and studied at Louisiana State University, Longwood College, and Bowling Green University, where she earned an M.F.A. She is now an assistant professor of English at Hollins College. She has published one collection of poems, *Blood, Hook & Eye*, in 1977, and is currently working on more poems, some short stories, and a novel.

JONATHAN WILLIAMS was born in Asheville, North Carolina, in 1929. Educated at St. Albans School, Princeton University, and Black Mountain College, he also studied art and design at the Institute of Design in Chicago. He is the executive director of the Jargon Society, Inc., of Highlands, North Carolina, a publishing company specializing in avant-garde poetry. He has been scholar-in-residence at three universities and has been a recipient of a Guggenheim Fellowship and several National Endowment for the Arts grants. Among his most representative titles are *The Empire Finals at Verona*, *Amen/Huzza/Selah*, and *Blues and Roots, Rue and Bluets*. A collection of his selected poems, *An Ear in Bartram's Tree*, was published in 1969.

MILLER WILLIAMS was born in 1930 in Hoxie, Arkansas. He has a B.S. degree in biology from Arkansas State College, and an M.S. in zoology from the University of Arkansas. He has taught biology and English at a number of southern colleges and is now professor of English at the University of Arkansas. He has been Fulbright professor of American studies at National University of Mexico and visiting professor, University of Chile, Santiago. In addition to his works as an editor and translator, he has published six books of poetry, including *The Only World There Is*, *Halfway from Hoxie: New and Selected Poems*, and *Why God Permits Evil*. He was awarded the Prix de Rome in 1976.

CHARLES WRIGHT was born in 1935 in Pickwick Dam, Tennessee. After graduating from Davidson College, he earned an M.A. at the University of Iowa. He has recently lived abroad and on the West Coast, where he is currently on the faculty at the University of California, Irvine. Among his four books of poetry are *Hard Freight*, *Bloodlines*, and *China Trace*, all in the Wesleyan series.

AL YOUNG was born in Ocean Springs, Mississippi, in 1939. He studied at the University of Michigan and Stanford University, and has an A.B. in Spanish from the University of California, Berkeley. Recipient of two National Endowment for the Arts grants and a Guggenheim Fellowship, he was also awarded a Wallace Stegner Writing Fellowship and a Joseph Henry Jackson Award. Once a freelance musician and a disc jockey, he has also been a creative writing teacher. His publications include novels, screenplays, and four volumes of poetry: *Dancing*, *The Song Turning Back into Itself*, *Some Recent Fiction*, and *Geography of the Near Past*. He is currently living near San Francisco and working on a novel.